Improvement Through Inspection?

Complementary Approaches to School Development

.EDITED BY

PETER EARLEY, BRIAN FIDLER
AND JANET OUSTON

David Fulton Publishers
London

David Fulton Publishers Ltd
2 Barbon Close, London WC1N 3JX

First published in Great Britain by David Fulton Publishers 1996

Note: The right of Peter Earley, Brian Fidler and Janet Ouston to be identified as the editors of this work has been asserted by them in accordance with the Copyright, Designs and Patents Act 1988.

Copyright © David Fulton Publishers Ltd

British Library Cataloguing in Publication Data

A catalogue record for this book is available from the British Library

ISBN 1-85346-407-4

Typeset by Textype Typesetters, Cambridge
Printed in Great Britain by BPC Books and Journals Ltd., Exeter

Contents

Contributors

Marie Brown is a lecturer in Educational Management and Administration and Head of the Centre for Continuing Professional Development in the Department of Education at Manchester University.

Gill Cleland was a deputy head in two comprehensive schools before becoming Senior Lecturer in Educational Management in the Centre for Educational Development at the University of Wolverhampton. She is also an OFSTED inspector.

Martin Corrick is a lecturer in the Department of Adult Continuing Education, University of Southampton. He has been involved in education as a teacher, writer, governor and governor training co-ordinator. His current interests include research and training in school governance.

Peter Earley worked for many years at the National Foundation for Educational Research undertaking a number of projects in the areas of school management and professional development. After a spell at the Institute of Education, University of London, he is now based at the Oxford Centre for Education Management, Oxford Brookes University.

Brian Fidler is Senior Lecturer and course leader of the 'Managing School Improvement' higher degree at the University of Reading. He has published widely in the field of school management; his most recent book is on strategic planning and school improvement.

Tony Hinkley is currently a deputy head of a comprehensive school in the West Midlands and an Associate Director of the Regional Staff College in Dudley.

Frances Kelly is currently Executive Assistant: Planning and Development at Auckland College of Education, New Zealand. She spent the 1994–1995 academic year as a Commonwealth Relations Trust Fellow at the Institute of Education University of London, carrying out a comparative study of external and internal quality assurance systems within higher, further and statutory education in England.

Janet Ouston is Senior Lecturer and Head of the Management Development Centre at the Institute of Education, University of London. A researcher in early school effectiveness studies, her current interests are on the impact of inspection and the applicability of 'quality approaches' to schools.

Keith Pocklington used to work at the NFER but for the last eight years has been an independent consultant (in partnership with Dick Weindling) with CREATE (Consultancy Research Evaluation and Training in Education). His recent publications include evaluations of a school improvement initiative (in a London borough) and the national head teacher mentoring scheme. He was also co-author of the 'Effective Management in Schools' project report, funded by the DFE.

Jane Seddon is Principal Director of the Regional Staff College in Dudley, West Midlands and an executive director of the British Deming Association. Amongst other things she is currently working with the BDA to co-ordinate Deming's work in schools nationally.

Louise Stoll is Senior Lecturer and Co-ordinating Director of the International School Effectiveness and Improvement Centre (ISEIC) at the Institute of Education, University of London. She has researched, written and presented widely on school improvement and effectiveness issues.

John Taylor is a freelance educational consultant in Management and Total Quality and 'Investors in People' in the Department of Education at Manchester University.

Peter Thomas has recently taken up the headship of a secondary school in South East England. After a period as a university researcher he taught in five large comprehensive schools and community colleges. Before teaching he trained in management and worked in industry.

Maureen Thomson, formerly a primary school headteacher, is Principal Adviser and head of the 'Whole School Improvement Centre' in Lewisham LEA's Quality Assurance and Development team. She is also an ISEIC Associate at the Institute of Education, University of London.

Dick Weindling previously worked at the NFER and is now a partner (with Keith Pocklington) of CREATE. In addition to the school improvement work, recent projects include national and local evaluations, and the 'Effective Management in Schools' project. He is currently working as a consultant with schools 'in need of special measures'.

Roger Whittaker is headteacher of St. Margaret's CE Junior School in Staffordshire, the first primary school in the county to receive the 'Investors in People' award.

Nick Zienau, formerly a director of the Community Education Unit in central London and an adviser with the ILEA, has for the past eight years traded as Zienau Consulting, based in Blackheath, London, specialising in process consultancy. Projects have encompassed work with LEAs and schools in the U.K. and a number of European-based assignments.

CHAPTER ONE

Introduction: OFSTED Inspections and School Development

by Peter Earley, Brian Fidler and Janet Ouston

The Education Reform Act of 1988 had major implications for schools in England and Wales, requiring greatly increased delegation of responsibilities (for finance, resources, staffing and pupil numbers) from the Local Education Authorities (LEAs) to the nation's schools and their independent governing bodies. At the same time the Act introduced a National Curriculum which was prescriptive in terms of the content, if not the delivery, of the curriculum as expressed in terms of subjects. The Government stated that the success of its reforms – and the last eight years has seen an abundance of education legislation – would largely depend on the capacity of each school to manage its own affairs and it placed great reliance on heads and senior staff as managers. Indeed, although about five per cent of schools 'opted out' of control of their Local Education Authorities – as permitted by legislation – the term 'self-managing institution' is now commonly used as the increased delegation of resources and responsibilities to all schools has continued.

All of these reforms have had a major impact on the role of the LEA, one of whose responsibilities had been to monitor and evaluate the operation of their schools. Although the 1944 Education Act had given LEAs the statutory right to inspect their schools, it was apparent that different authorities were giving differing degrees of emphasis to this function with many preferring to work with schools in an 'advisory' rather than an 'inspectorial' capacity (Maychell and Keys 1993). Her Majesty's Inspectorate (HMI) also had a role in reporting on individual schools but limited resources and a brief that went beyond inspection to include disseminating good practice and providing data to inform national policy making, meant that most schools did not experience a 'visitation' on a regular basis. In 1991, for example, HMI 'published reports on two per cent of primary schools (a 50 year inspection cycle) and ten per cent of secondary schools (a ten year inspection cycle)' (Riches 1992). Indeed, many heads and staff speak of never having experienced a full HMI inspection.

The 1992 Education Act not only reduced considerably the size and role of HMI but brought into existence the Office for Standards in Education (OFSTED). This was established – and funded primarily from resources that hitherto had been allocated to LEAs – to do two main things:

- to devise a framework for school inspections
- to oversee a system of four-yearly inspections of schools.

The OFSTED style of external inspection marked a radical change from the past in a number of important ways:

- it was based on an explicit framework – the *Handbook for the Inspection of Schools* publishes explicit criteria for the inspection as well as outlining a standardised inspection procedure;
- it required extensive classroom observation;
- it was undertaken by a team of independent inspectors, trained for the task and working to a contract;
- each team was led by a Registered Inspector and required to include a 'lay' person;
- it required the school to produce an 'action plan' in response to the main issues identified in the OFSTED inspectors' report;
- special measures were to follow in schools reported as unsatisfactory or 'at risk'.

The *Handbook* made clear that the purpose of the inspection report was:

an appraisal of the quality and standards of education in the school and some descriptive detail is obviously necessary, but the emphasis throughout should be on judgements and evaluation .... The function of the report is to evaluate, not to prescribe or speculate; reports must be as objective as possible. (OFSTED 1993, p17)

More recently OFSTED has stated that the intention of inspection is to:

... promote school improvement by identifying priorities for action, and to inform parents and the local community about a school's strengths and weaknesses. (OFSTED 1995a, p2)

The purpose of the inspection is to report on four main areas, which are spelt out in great detail in the OFSTED *Handbook*, namely:

- the educational standards achieved in the school;
- the quality of education provided by the school;
- whether the resources available to the school were managed efficiently;
- the spiritual, moral, social and cultural development of students at the school.

The inspection of the first cohort of secondary schools began in Autumn 1993 with primary school inspections commencing a year later. The original inspection *Framework* was modified in Autumn 1993, Spring 1994 and again after a consultation exercise in 1995, so that a revised *Framework* was introduced to be used in schools from the Summer of 1996. There have been a number of changes of a minor nature but an important one – introduced after the consultation exercise and yet to be published at the time of writing – was to give a greater emphasis on the school's capacity to monitor and evaluate progress towards its priorities and targets. OFSTED inspections were now to include an assessment of the school's capability to manage change and review its own systems for institutional development. The inspection was to pay greater attention to a school's own evaluation of its strengths and weaknesses. It stated in the new draft *Framework* that schools would be expected to monitor and evaluate their performance, systematically and regularly, and 'seek to improve (their) effectiveness, taking into account the impact of any quality assurance measures adopted' (OFSTED 1995a, p24). OFSTED's *Update Number 15* states that the revised *Framework* aims to: make inspection more manageable by inspectors; more acceptable and useful to schools; contribute more effectively to schools' strategies for sustained improvement and to result in better evaluation and reporting (p1).

The findings of each school inspection contribute to the annual report of Her Majesty's Chief Inspector of Schools to the Secretary of State for Education. Of more significance to the inspected school, however, is the legal requirement for it – or strictly speaking its governing body – to produce an Action Plan, dealing with the identified 'key issues for action'. It was primarily through this mechanism but also through preparation for inspection and the inspection process itself, that the main aim of OFSTED – as expressed by its logo – *Improvement through Inspection* – was to be achieved. How successful OFSTED has been in achieving its aim is the subject of much debate.

This book similarly has as its central focus *school development* or *school improvement* as it has increasingly become known. However, the main concern of the book is not the inspectorial mode or that of external audit but rather to explore a variety of different ways in which schools and colleges are attempting to examine their own practices with a view to improving the quality of teaching and learning. In this respect it should be particularly useful to schools considering the various approaches to institutional self-evaluation and review, which as noted earlier, is an important theme in the revised OFSTED *Framework*.

This book should be seen as a companion volume to another set of contributions compiled by the editors which offers a critique of the OFSTED model, whilst also bringing together the main findings of the most significant research studies to date into the inspection process (Ouston, Fidler and Earley 1996a). The first contribution in this (second) book – by one of the editors, Peter Earley – summarises the latest research evidence on the role of the OFSTED inspection in the process of school improvement. It shows that there is a growing body of research – albeit much of it from OFSTED itself – pointing to the important role that external inspection can play but stresses that none of this research is considering the relative cost-effectiveness of this model or investigating alternatives. It also points to the clear dichotomy (and confusion) that exists between perceptions of OFSTED's accountability role and that of school 'improvement through inspection', and concludes by suggesting a number of important areas in need of further research.

The next two chapters take school improvement as their central theme but offer different routes for schools to consider. The authors of the first – Louise Stoll from the International School Effectiveness and Improvement Centre, at the Institute of Education, University of London, and Maureen Thomson of Lewisham LEA – give an account of a project they have been involved in over several years working with schools in South London. The approach to school development outlined is one of partnership and emphasises the need for schools to operate with others – schools, LEAs and universities – in order to develop 'critical friendships' whilst empowering participants. Stoll and Thomas make extensive use of the school effectiveness and school improvement literature, both from this country and North America, to discuss the various strategies that can be used to 'open the doors to school improvement'. They document one primary school's experiences in the Lewisham project to discuss the partnership model in action. Its key elements they see as shared beliefs, collaboration, support, joint evaluation and critical friendship.

Keith Pocklington and Dick Weindling, from the CREATE consultancy, whilst also looking to North America, draw on a different literature to explain the origins of the approach they have been using for their work with schools. Their chapter provides an interesting contrast to that by Stoll and Thomas, emphasising as they do the focus of their work in 'organisational development' (OD) and reminding us of the first use (and meaning) of the term 'action research'. Their account of working with five schools in two LEAs, provides useful insights into many of the constraints and limitations which confront 'process' consultants and advisers as they attempt to implement change programmes with an improvement focus. The school improvement strategy they outline involves four overlapping phases: entry and start up; review and needs assessment; planning and implementation; and monitoring, review and evaluation. Pocklington and Weindling describe their experiences of using this approach with secondary schools to draw out the key messages about implementing school improvement programmes.

Approaches to 'OD' as outlined by Pocklington and Weindling have their origins outside of education as do many of the so-called 'quality initiatives' currently found in industry and commerce, and beginning to impact on education. (A useful discussion of the different approaches to quality and their applicability to education is found in Parsons 1994.) The next six chapters are all concerned with various aspects of these initiatives. Tony Hinkley and Jane Seddon from the Regional Management Centre in the West Midlands, draw upon their current work with schools involved with the British Deming Association, to offer some observations of the approach to school development commonly referred to as 'Total Quality Management' – a term, as they remind us, not actually used by Deming himself. They show clearly how such an approach to school development is extremely critical of external accountability models of 'quality control' and they provide some useful pointers to a viable alternative.

Janet Ouston is also supportive of such an approach to school development. Before outlining the essential characteristics and potential benefits to schools of a quality approach, she offers a critique of what might be termed the school effectiveness movement, suggesting that its value is limited. It is argued that there is now a need to look elsewhere for more useful models and frameworks for school development, particularly in terms of understanding the various processes that promote change and development. It is the processes underpinning organisational development that are important and both Ouston's and Hinkley and Seddon's contributions helpfully remind us of Deming's recurring question 'by what means?' – a theme picked up by some of the other contributors.

Gill Cleland is also interested in quality approaches and she outlines a system of management review and improvement designed for school management teams. She draws upon the school effectiveness literature but also that on effective school management to examine the characteristics of effective team and organisational management, which, she argues, are essential components of quality management systems. Cleland and her colleagues at the University of Wolverhampton have designed a competence-based approach to management development which can be used for individual and organisational development. Cleland's chapter refers to the work she has piloted and evaluated in relation to senior team development in primary schools in the West Midlands, although it is clear that the approach could be used with the secondary sector. Interestingly, this approach to management team development grew out of a competence-based individual accredited programme developed at the University and was instigated partly in response to senior managers' concerns to review management processes and develop improvement strategies in the light of forthcoming OFSTED inspections. Managers were concerned to be able to supply evidence of 'the school's use of self-evaluation and analysis' (OFSTED 1993 pp33–34), which, as stated earlier, is given even greater importance in the revised *Framework*.

The next three chapters focus on 'Investors in People' and provide insights into the applicability and usefulness of this particular quality initiative. 'Investors in People' is a Government initiated scheme, administered through Training and Enterprise Councils (TECs), which provides a set of standards or benchmarks in relation to training and development, against which organisations can ascertain their effectiveness. The National Standard consists of four principles or statements focusing on commitment, planning, action and evaluation. Each principle is accompanied by a number of indicators – 24 in total – and evidence gathered in order to assess whether or not the organisation can gain formal recognition as an 'Investor in People'. (The Appendix to this book outlines the 24 indicators of the Standard which will be used in accreditation.)

Unlike some of the other industry-derived quality initiatives (such as BS 5750 or ISO 9000), 'Investors in People' has been seen by many schools as potentially of great value. At the time of writing about 2,400 companies and 85 schools had gained recognition as 'Investors' with nearly 1,100 schools having made formal commitments to work towards becoming an 'Investor in People'. To achieve the Standard normally takes about two years and experience has shown that it need *not* be a rigid, bureaucratic or paper-driven exercise – the process is about 'Investing in People' not 'Investing in Paper'! It has been said to bring many benefits to organisations – and the three chapters highlight what these might be – and yet is difficult if not impossible to achieve without effective management. The following chapters discuss how this initiative has impacted on schools and point to the possible ways it leads to improvement in organisational and individual performance.

Schools have taken to this voluntary initiative for a number of reasons, one of which, most probably, has been the subsidies provided by the TECs. (This has been linked to the fact that achieving 'Investors in People' is part of the Government's national education and training targets or NETTS – see Chapter 8.) Indeed, an interesting issue in the future will be the extent to which schools are prepared to fund the real cost of consultants and, perhaps more importantly, the assessment process. For some schools formal recognition has been less of a priority; it has been the processes underpinning 'Investors' that are said to have brought the major benefits.

Initial evaluations and feedback from schools and TECs suggest four key issues are commonly found or need to be addressed:

- evaluation – an area in which most schools need to give greater attention;
- support staff – a major pay-off as most schools have traditionally not attended to the needs of non-teaching staff;
- the potential conflict between individual development needs and those of the school ('Investors' focuses on the latter) has not created problems;
- the role of middle managers – 'Investors' has reaffirmed the need for middle managers to embrace fully their staff development responsibilities.

These and other issues are further explored in Chapters 8, 9 and 10, and crucial questions are being raised about whether the Standard can be achieved without implications for the management of schools. Also, involvement in 'Investors' means the notion of the school as a 'learning organisation' is being brought to the fore. What is clear, however, is that as self-managing institutions schools will operate more in the employer role and greater attention will need to be given to the management of staff development and developing the roles of managers, particularly staff development co-ordinators (Earley 1995). The training materials produced by Understanding British Industry (UBI) specifically for schools interested in examining their training and development function should prove helpful here.

The first contribution on 'Investors in People' is by Nick Zienau, a freelance consultant who has worked with over 40 schools in south east London. He draws on this experience and that of his consultant colleagues to give an informed critique of the potential of 'Investors' for achieving school improvement. The chapter focuses specifically on a number of process issues around consultancy and organisational development. Zienau shows how the consultancy work they are currently engaged in is facilitating change, but more importantly, enabling schools to change themselves by tackling issues around such notions as organisational culture, process and resistance. Reference is made to two basic hypotheses about the implementation of change – the rational model and the existential model – and, it is argued, consultants are in a strong position to assist schools to address the change process, particularly regarding the latter, more common model. The notion of the reflective and skilled practitioner, Zienau argues, applies to both the consultant as well as to the professionals working in schools.

The next chapter on 'Investors in People' is by Marie Brown and John Taylor of the School of Education, University of Manchester. They describe the work they have been doing as trainers and consultants with a group of primary schools in Staffordshire. Interestingly, the schools' involvement in 'Investors' came out of a one day course designed to inform primary school senior managers of the implications of OFSTED inspections! Brown and Taylor talk of the potential benefits to schools in terms of improved performance; increased motivation, commitment and loyalty; greater customer satisfaction; and organisational reputation. Their work in a cluster of primary schools leads them to make a number of generalisations, relating to such areas as support staff, planning, clarity of purpose, climate or culture, appraisal, ownership of the process and school management. This chapter also includes a personal view from Roger Whittaker, one of the primary school head teachers involved in the project, who talks very positively of the benefits gained, particularly in relation to such matters as staff appraisal and school development planning.

In a similar but more detailed way, Peter Thomas relays his experiences over the last two years as a deputy head in a secondary school who was given responsibility to implement 'Investors'. He describes how an audit was undertaken of the school's 'culture in use' against the Standard's 24 assessment indicators through both documentary analysis and an analysis of processes for managing people – or human resource management (HRM) as he prefers to call it. As a result it was apparent that there were a number of gaps between current practice and that required of the Standard. These shortfalls were included in the targets of the school's Development Plan and senior staff took responsibility for bringing about the necessary improvements. Through the use of force-field analysis a number of barriers were identified which were seen as preventing the development of the school's HRM practices. Staff perception questionnaires provided further evidence that key opinion leaders were not totally committed to the initiative. Thomas lists the main fears staff held (such as concern over initiative overload) and that for some the notion of a corporate culture – which underpins 'Investors' – was anathema. A plan was developed over the next 18 months or so in order to try to 'win over' the opponents and obtain the 'critical mass' needed for successful implementation. The commitment plan attempted to address issues of organisational culture, structure and process. Finally, Thomas reflects on some of the costs and benefits to the school and concludes by pointing to the contribution 'Investors' can make to school improvement. The evidence from Thomas's school is that the initiative does have the potential to be a key element in quality management systems and continuous organisational improvement.

Martin Corrick – a former LEA governor trainer currently working in adult and continuing education at the University of Southampton – considers the role of the governing body in school development. In a challenging essay Corrick attempts to explain how governors can contribute to their schools by drawing on the most recent research into governance and school management. It is interesting to note that the school effectiveness literature makes no reference to governing bodies, although some of the commonly mentioned characteristics or correlates of effective schools, such as home–school partnerships, could be said to be applicable to governors (Sammons, Hillman and Mortimore 1995). Is this state of affairs largely because 'gubernatorial matters' have not been seen as sufficiently important to warrant such research or is it simply an oversight on the part of the researchers? Whatever the explanation, Corrick argues that governing bodies have an important part to play in both school development and accountability but to date their role has, in general, been somewhat restricted. Their potential however should not be underestimated and the chapter provides an interesting analysis of how the role might be developed in order for governing bodies to become effective.

The following chapter, by one of the editors, provides a review of recent research conducted into school development planning and strategic planning. The latter is increasingly being used as a term in schools but rarely to mean little more than long-term planning. Brian Fidler clarifies the distinguishing features of strategy, outlines the potential benefits of strategic and development planning, and points to some of the difficulties and limitations that researchers are highlighting. Various forms of planning, including post-OFSTED action planning, are currently high on many educationists' agendas and there is a need to understand and gain insights into best practice in relation to school development.

In the final chapter, before the editors' concluding comments, Frances Kelly provides an alternative perspective based on her year as a Commonwealth Research Trust Fellow at the Institute of Education, University of London. Her interest is in institutional approaches to self-review and by examining quality assurance practices in the higher and further education sectors in the United Kingdom she offers alternatives to the OFSTED model for consideration. As Kelly notes, the 'audit explosion' (Power 1994) is upon us; the challenge is, however, to ensure that it leads to real improvements in educational outcomes and processes. She identifies the importance of self-assessment – which, as earlier noted, has now been incorporated within the revised OFSTED *Framework* – and quality assurance by peer review. The former, Kelly suggests, cannot on its own provide a valid measure for accountability but it is a major factor in quality improvement. Similarly, peer review can have significant benefits, particularly in staff development terms. External audits, although primarily about accountability, do provide schools and colleges with an independent and objective analysis of their strengths and weaknesses. Kelly suggests that what is needed are further comparative studies of the

10

various models of external assessment to determine the most effective way to provide accountability, while fostering institutional quality improvement. Improvement efforts can be based on audits – both internal and external – and critical self-review, ultimately so that educational establishments become better places both for their students and for those who work in them.

CHAPTER TWO

School Improvement and OFSTED Inspection: the Research Evidence

by Peter Earley

As shown in the accompanying volume to this book, there is a growing body of research into various aspects of the OFSTED inspection process (Ouston, Fidler and Earley 1996a). Very little of this research, however, has addressed the key question of whether or not inspections, as currently conducted, have a significant role to play in school improvement or development. There are, of course, good reasons for this dearth of research evidence on this crucial issue, the most important of which relates to the time frame. Change, particularly that which impacts on the quality of teaching and learning, does not happen overnight and the current system of external inspection, conducted by privatised teams of inspectors contracted by OFSTED, has been in existence only since Autumn 1993 (see Chapter 1).

Nevertheless, a detailed and systematic analysis of the specific role of OFSTED inspections in school development is crucial for several reasons. Of most obvious significance is the cost of the exercise – estimated to be over £100m per annum or about £30,000 for an average-sized secondary school. But also of significance is the fact that OFSTED perceives its own role as 'fundamentally concerned with securing improvement' (OFSTED 1993). Indeed, OFSTED's logo, from which this book has taken its title, is *'Improvement through Inspection'*. The key questions which therefore need to be asked are: is it working and, if so, is it cost-effective and does it represent value for money? This chapter draws on existing research to try and answer the first question. It concludes by raising a number of issues that require further research, including the need for some kind of 'cost-benefit' analysis of the whole inspection process.

It should be noted that OFSTED sees its role with regard to school improvement in two main ways. Improvement through inspection has to include both what happens at the individual school level and in the education system at large as a result of inspection (Matthews and Smith 1995). OFSTED has a broader role, as did Her Majesty's Inspectorate (HMI), to advise the Secretary of State and to produce an annual report on the nation's schools. The concern of this chapter, however, is with the first meaning of the term; that is the impact the inspection process has on schools and their development. It is intended to investigate the effects of OFSTED inspections on those schools – the vast majority – which are not deemed to be in need of 'special measures' or 'failing to provide pupils with an appropriate standard of education'. In order to do this reference will be made to the ongoing BEMAS (British Educational Management and Administration Society) research conducted by the editors and to the growing research-based literature emerging from OFSTED itself.

Enquiries by OFSTED

To OFSTED's credit, attempts have been made to monitor the effects of inspection and to review the value of the inspection process itself. Disentangling the effects of inspection from the myriad of other changes affecting schools over recent years is, however, one of the first difficulties confronted by researchers. Yet, as two senior OFSTED officers rightly state, 'whether OFSTED's programme contributes to school improvement has to be established, rather than simply asserted' (Matthews and Smith 1995). They suggest that there is growing evidence that 'the introduction of the inspection system, together with post-inspection action planning, is making a contribution to school improvement' (p29). On the basis of surveys of secondary schools undertaken by OFSTED they claim that the major benefits of inspection include:

- the value of having an external audit of achievements, strengths and weaknesses, providing information for parents and accountability for the expenditure of public money;
- the growth in confidence and morale resulting from affirmation of a school's quality and direction;
- the major impetus provided to focus thinking on aspects of the school which did not meet the *Framework* criteria and its power to act as a catalyst to accelerate policy review and staff development;
- the identification of areas for improvement, although some inspection reports still need to make these more clear. (Matthews and Smith 1995, p30)

The main platform on which developments will take place is seen as largely through the identification of 'key issues for action' and the 'Action Plan' that is produced in response to the inspection. Action Plans have to be written within 40 working days of the publication of the inspection report and schools have been given guidance on their production (DFE Circular 7/93). OFSTED claim that many of the more straightforward issues have been implemented and a sample of Action Plans have been monitored over the first year.

The action planning process certainly has the potential for achieving significant change. As the author of a practical guide to post-OFSTED action planning notes:

> ... it holds within it the seeds of successful improvement. Pragmatically, and not inappropriately, the process of action planning deals with issues one at a time, and sets out the actions to be taken by individuals and small groups. (Russell 1994)

What is more, it is stated that Action Plans can affect the school as a place to work in:

> It can increasingly become one where the culture amongst staff supports reflection and the improvement of teaching skills; one where people can be open about successes and failures; one where concerns and complaints can be raised ... sometimes the mere process of inspection brings staff closer together and begins to make changes. (Russell 1994, p58)

Russell is also clear, however, that the process of inspection is not the most certain way of improving a school as:

> ... such a comprehensive external audit, reporting to general criteria applied across all institutions, carries the risk of leading to sterile conclusions which will be followed by no real change. (Russell 1994, p57)

What then do we know about the action planning process? Has it led to improvements in schools in the longer term?

In 1994 OFSTED published two reports which provide some insights into inspection and the action planning process. The first, entitled *Planning Improvement: Schools' Post-Inspection Action Plans* was undertaken by HMI (the professional arm of OFSTED) and based on a survey of a representative sample of 85 (mainly secondary) schools inspected in 1993–4. Visits were made to schools, interviews conducted with heads, teachers and governors, inspection reports read and Action Plans scrutinised. In addition, data were obtained from 15 schools which had serious weaknesses or which required special measures (OFSTED 1995b, p1).

The above report's prime purpose was to help and inform those responsible for preparing and implementing Action Plans. It notes that the success of the process will be influenced by the school's approach to inspection and the degree to which inspection is perceived as contributing to school evaluation and development. After noting the essential features of the best Action Plans, reference is made to the survey which found that 'governing bodies and their schools have responded positively to the requirement to produce a post-OFSTED action plan' (OFSTED 1995b, p3). The main findings from the survey, which are worth stating in full, were that the majority of schools had:

- addressed all of the key issues from the inspection (96%);
- made adequate preparation for their action plans (91%), which in a third of schools enabled work to commence on the plan before receipt of the published report;
- set out a clear timetable and identified the person responsible for each aspect (74%); and
- made discernible progress at an early stage in tackling some of the key issues in a way that was leading or likely to lead to improvement, by taking measures to improve teaching, raise expectations, address underachievement or ensure that pupils had more positive attitudes to their work (61%).

The report went on to state that the survey found few schools had:

- set specific targets for improvement of achievement (4%);
- developed criteria or indicators against which to monitor and evaluate the effectiveness of the proposed action in terms of raised standards (8%); or
- assessed the full costs of resources to implement the plan (6%). (OFSTED 1995b, pp3-4)

Finally, although not the focus of this chapter, it is interesting to note that the survey found that schools with 'serious weaknesses' did not receive sufficient support to produce an effective Action Plan, whilst those requiring 'special measures' were given substantial assistance (from their LEAs) in the action planning process.

The second OFSTED research-based report, published at about the same time – *Inspection Quality, 1994/1995* – was a review of the inspection system itself. This was a follow-up to the earlier *A Focus on Quality* (OFSTED 1994b) which had reviewed the first 100 secondary school inspections in autumn 1993. The second review – undertaken by OFSTED itself, with external validation of the findings (and independent commentary) from the management consultants Touche Ross and the University of Keele – had as its main focus the operation of inspection in the primary, special and nursery school sectors. The review also followed up the progress of secondary school inspections and made a number of comments concerning OFSTED's role in school improvement.

The review of primary, nursery and special schools was based on data collected in a variety of ways. The main survey consisted of 100 one day visits by HMI, when discussions were held with key participants, including parents and pupils. In addition a postal survey of 242 schools (response rate of less than 50 per cent) which had been inspected but not visited by HMI was conducted, where points raised were used to validate the findings from the 100 visits. A postal survey of Registered, team and Lay inspectors (n=523) was also carried out. The OFSTED report also included findings from visits to 100 secondary schools and a survey of Action Plans from a representative sample of 69 secondary schools, 12 primary and four special schools. (It is this latter data set of 85 schools which formed the basis of the *Planning Improvement* document described above.)

The main findings of the *Inspection Quality* report, which are of most relevance here, were that the majority of heads found the inspection preparation an effective team-building exercise which provided the opportunity for self-review. Under half of the teachers were satisfied with the amount and nature of the professional dialogue shared with inspectors. There was found to be a general satisfaction with most aspects of oral feedback to senior managers and governors, although many teachers requested more detailed information on subjects and were less satisfied with the oral feedback. Greatest dissatisfaction was reported when feedback to teachers lacked detail or was too brief. The Key Issues section of the inspectors' reports was seen as providing a sound basis for future action but it was felt there was scope for making it more useful. At times the key issues were said to lack clarity or not to have been the subject of detailed discussions during feedback (OFSTED 1995c).

It is interesting that the commentary on the post-inspection phase (by Paul Fuller from Touche Ross and Michael Barber from Keele) notes that 'the quality of feedback, both oral and written, is likely to be an important determinant of whether inspection is followed by improvement' (p25). They also comment that it is important for inspection reports to give credit to schools where things are done well, not only because it offers a more rounded picture but also as it means the school is more likely to take seriously any criticisms that might be reported, and, presumably, therefore more likely to act on them. They go on to note that as many as one half of the schools had at least some concerns about the validity of the key issues identified by the inspectors and remark:

> … furthermore, as a result of some detailed follow-up, it is possible to suggest that schools with critical reports are more likely to have concerns about the validity of the conclusions. While on one level this is hardly surprising, it implies that those schools with most to do following an inspection, are precisely those least likely to accept the agenda set out in the Key Issues section of the report. (OFSTED 1995c, p26)

The fourth section of the *Inspection Quality* report talks of further developments in the inspection of secondary schools. Mention is made of visits to 100 secondary schools inspected in the first year (1993/1994), and the benefits of the inspection system were seen by the schools to be twofold.

1. Secondary schools saw many advantages in a national system.

Many accept that independent inspection has an important part to play in ensuring greater accountability, and acknowledge the value of having a comprehensive audit of their strengths and weaknesses. They are reassured by the system's objectivity, not least because inspection is based on the clear and open criteria published in the *Framework for Inspection*. (OFSTED 1995c, p29)

2. Schools had a high expectation of the potential for improvement and development afforded by inspection.

Indeed inspection is often valued most where inspectors are willing to engage in professional dialogue to promote development. The great majority of schools feel the *Framework* and *Handbook* are important tools that can be used to support a range of management functions such as self-review, development planning, staff development and appraisal. (OFSTED 1995c, pp29–30)

The report goes on to add that although the bulk of schools are generally satisfied with their inspection and appreciate its comprehensive nature, there was some concern that:

... the inspection of some important contributory factors, such as management, tends to produce superficial (though not necessarily unsound) judgements which fail to identify where development or improvement could or should be made. Schools expect that inspection findings should advance their thinking, and not simply confirm current practice and established priorities. (OFSTED 1995c, p30)

It notes that some of the 'Key Issues for Action' which have to be addressed in the post-OFSTED Action Plan were said to lack clarity and precision, whilst others were seen as 'too peripheral to promote significant improvements in school performance' (p31). Recent guidance for the writing of Key Issues for Action states that they should normally be few in number, be specific to the school and be listed in order of significance.

Finally, in the last section of the report many of the findings from the *Planning Improvement* document are outlined, and the importance of target-setting is noted, particularly in terms of raising standards of achievement. Clearly defined Action Plans 'contained strategies to promote higher achievement'. Yet as stated:

... it was too early at the time of the survey to observe improvement in standards of achievement but many schools were able to show that they had clear strategies for addressing this issue. (OFSTED 1995c, p33)

Unsurprisingly, schools which drew upon successful experience of development planning were found to be more effective at implementing Action Plans and the process of action planning was seen as supporting and strengthening aspects of self-review already adopted. OFSTED reports that:

> ... in the most effective practice the period of preparation for inspection and action planning became assimilated into the school's own mechanisms for monitoring standards and improving the quality of provision. The legal requirement to produce an annual report on the implementation of the action plan underlines the importance of schools adopting a systematic approach to the monitoring and evaluation of their improvement. (OFSTED 1995c, p33)

In the introduction to the report, Fuller and Barber make several poignant comments about the contribution of OFSTED inspections to school improvement. They remark that given OFSTED's emphasis on 'Improvement through Inspection' it is important to consider the extent to which it is occurring and note that the data presented:

> ... suggests that the great majority of schools inspected had incorporated the key issues for action in their action plans and made discernible progress towards implementation. Ultimately the success of the inspection process will depend upon its impact judged in terms of its effects on levels of pupil achievement measured through examination results, tests and other means but, at this stage, it remains too early to study its impact in this respect. (OFSTED 1995c, p4)

The authors go on to remark that although 'Improvement through inspection' is 'an emerging reality', the more difficult question 'is whether the present process maximises the improvement that might result from inspection'. They point to school self-review in preparation for inspection as being highly beneficial and the need for this aspect of the inspection to be enhanced. Similarly, they note the possible need for changes to be made 'to ensure that follow-up to inspection is more effective than it has been to date' (p5). Indeed, an important recent change has been the introduction of training grants (GEST category 1, School Effectiveness) which can be spent in relation to the post-OFSTED Action Plan.

The BEMAS research

The final evidence base that will be drawn upon in order to explore further the key issue of school improvement through external inspection is that of the BEMAS research conducted by the editors. The origins of this research and its findings are outlined in detail in the accompanying volume (Ouston, Fidler and Earley 1996b). The following account therefore summarises the main findings only.

The research collected data on the initial cohort of secondary schools inspected in the Autumn Term 1993 by the use of a questionnaire – usually completed by the head teacher – and a small number of case studies (4), during which interviews were conducted with heads, senior and middle managers and chairs of governors. The three main research questions were:

- Did schools find the inspection helpful in their own development?
- What was the relationship between the Action Plan and the School Development Plan?
- How could the inspection process help schools in a more effective and efficient way?

Data were collected at least two terms after the inspection when each school had produced its Action Plan. Views were sought on how schools prepared for inspection, their assessment of the value of the verbal debriefing received at the end of the inspection, and the value of the final written report which the school received six weeks after the inspection. Responses were received from 170 schools, a response rate of 60 per cent.

In broad terms, the schools said that the final report from the inspectors made slightly more contribution to school development than did either the verbal feedback or the preparation for the inspection. Nevertheless, all three phases – pre-inspection, the inspection itself and the report – were seen by the majority as being of some benefit. Only about six per cent of the sample were quite negative about the contribution that the OFSTED inspection process had made to their school's development. Schools that found one of these phases helpful in contributing to school development were also likely to report the other phases as helpful. The opposite was also found to be the case with those schools finding one phase of little value reporting similarly for the other two phases.

The research also found that those schools who reported the inspection being most useful to their own development were those where there was a moderate overlap between the Action Plan and their Development Plan (SDP). Schools where there was some overlap between the two were much more positive than those where the action points were already included in the school's Plan. Schools that could envisage ways of using the inspection process were more likely to report positively on its value. Also the research showed that in those schools where inspection was said to have had a major contribution to development, the governing body was involved in drawing up the Action Plan as were external advisers (Ouston, Fidler and Earley 1996b)

The researchers have followed up this group of schools first inspected in the Autumn Term 1993 to investigate their perceptions of the impact of inspection two years later. This research with the original cohort of secondary schools sought views regarding the developmental role of

OFSTED inspections and whether or not Action Plans were being implemented in the way envisaged by OFSTED. Progress on the inspectors' 'issues for action' and other improvements made were also explored. Initial analyses suggest a positive picture emerging with nearly three-quarters of respondents noting that the impact of the inspection on the development of the school has been 'very positive' or 'positive'. It is very likely that our follow-up sample is not entierely representsive however, and we are currently undertaking further analysis to ascertain if this is the case. The full results of this research will be published at a later date.

The second aspect of the follow-up study has been completed and the initial findings published (Fidler, Earley and Ouston 1995). This study was a replica of the first and sought the views of schools inspected one year later (i.e. in the Autumn Term 1994). Again, about 60 per cent of schools responded to our request for information which was made towards the end of the Summer Term 1995. The questionnaire was a modified version of that used earlier and some additional information was collected. An analysis of the data showed some interesting differences but many similarities to the initial BEMAS study.

Whereas in 1994 almost a quarter of schools had used an external consultant or inspector to give guidance on the state of the school pre-inspection, in 1995 this figure had risen to 38 per cent. The value of preparation was seen as much higher for the second group of schools (48%) than it was for the first (36%), with the mean response (on a five-point scale) going up from 2.9 to 3.28. A number of heads indicated that they had used the *Framework* to prepare their schools for inspection and had obviously found it of value. This reflects Matthews and Smith's (1995) and OFSTED's (1994c) view that the *Framework* was being used as a tool for school self-evaluation.

The mean figure for the value of verbal feedback for school development remained essentially the same at 2.93 (compared to 2.96), whilst the value of the final report fell from 3.16 to 3.01. In view of the slight decline in the value of the other two parts of the process the increase in the value of preparation is the more remarkable.

A previously unexplored issue which the case studies had highlighted was the effect of the inspection on the speed of development. The second survey found the range of effects to be quite high. Four per cent of respondents remarked that development had stopped in the school, with about a quarter stating it had slowed. Just over a third said it had speeded up, with the remainder – the largest single group (38%) – stating that it had been unaffected. Some respondents explained that the process of preparing for the inspection had prevented developments they wished to make, whilst others noted it had led them to make developments earlier than they might otherwise have done so. The reaction seemed to be both a function of the state of the school and also how the school perceived the inspection process. The latter was likely to be influenced by the school's reaction to the report and this was found to vary from the dispirited to the encouraged. The greatest number – nearly seven out of ten – were encouraged to varying degrees and this view was said to be shared by staff in the vast majority of cases.

Although the Action Plan is referred to as the 'governors' action plan', the earlier 1994 survey found that almost one half of respondents commented that the governing body played little or no part in its creation. The second survey in 1995 showed evidence of a little more involvement by governors in the production of action plans, whilst the contribution of consultants and the LEA remained virtually the same.

Finally, the 1994 survey found that 29 per cent of respondents stated that their Action Plans were coincident with their school's SDP or almost so, whereas the figure for 1995 was 55 per cent. In terms of the Action Plans and the SDPs being very different, the figures fell from 17 per cent to 5 per cent. The means on a five-point scale (where 5 indicated total incompatibility) were 1.52 in 1995 and 2.33 in 1994. These figures can be interpreted in two main ways: (a) as schools moving to standardise with OFSTED's priorities as Hargreaves (1995a) predicted, or (b) as changes to the SDP are made as preparation for OFSTED highlights some areas requiring urgent attention.

It should be emphasised that the above findings are based on the perceptions – usually head teacher perceptions – of the impact of OFSTED inspections on school development. We have no independent evidence of improvement having occured. Other things being equal, however, a favourable reaction to the inspection process would be more helpful than a negative one (OFSTED 1995b). Our research suggests that there are at least five factors influencing the responses:

- the state of education in the school
- the management processes in the school
- the attitude of the head teacher to inspection
- the inspection process, and
- the inspection findings.

As we note:

> Some of these factors are inter-related and, in addition, the state of the other factors will influence the outcome. The inspection process, both in terms of content and in terms of manner of being carried out, affects some factors directly and others indirectly. (Fidler, Earley and Ouston 1995)

The latest survey provides evidence of the positive impact of the present inspection process but the process itself could be improved. Clearly there are many areas in need of further, more detailed research.

The need for further research

It is clear that, to date, the research undertaken into the OFSTED inspection process and its contribution to school development has largely been undertaken by OFSTED itself. With the possible exception of the work of Gray and Wilcox (1995) and Shaw and colleagues (Shaw, Brimblecombe and Ormston 1995), there has been no independent research commissioned by an outside body to investigate the role of OFSTED inspections in *school improvement*. Gray and Wilcox have completed a follow-up study of a small number of schools (inspected by LEAs prior to the introduction of OFSTED but using the first OFSTED framework), whilst the Oxford Brookes University study has investigated teachers' perceptions of inspection and its potential for improvement in professional practice (Shaw, Brimblecombe and Ormston 1995).

Similarly, there has been no research conducted into the key question, raised by Hargreaves (1995a) and others, as to whether or not OFSTED inspections represent value for money. The answer to this question may depend on whether OFSTED's role is seen largely in terms of public accountability or school development, but there is a need for a detailed cost-benefit analysis of OFSTED inspections. Is there, for example, a more cost-effective way of identifying the small minority of 'failing' schools and 'those in need of special measures' and are we correct in assuming the inspection process has most developmental impact on such schools? Similarly, what would schools be doing if they were not preparing for inspection and what are the consequences of inspection for the pupils? Does their teaching and learning suffer in the short term as a result? Also, does the so-called 'post-inspection blues' have major deleterious effects on both the pupils and the development of the school?

The bulk of the research currently being undertaken, especially that by OFSTED itself, does not question the OFSTED *Framework* or the rationale behind such an approach to school improvement. OFSTED's own enquiries are, perhaps understandably, conducted within their own conceptual framework and attempt to answer predominantly their own questions. The focus is on how the system is working, not whether it should be working as it is. There is, therefore, a need to go beyond that framework and to investigate alternative approaches to inspection and improvement. Also, as several university professors have recently argued (Hofkins 1995), there is a need to conduct independent evaluations of OFSTED itself, investigating amongst other things, its claims to validity and reliability.

We await with interest therefore the outcomes of the Chief Inspector's recent statement that a research study is to be commissioned to evaluate the impact of inspection and action planning on school improvement (OFSTED 1995d). In addition, there are plans to ascertain the kind of external support that is most useful to schools when they are responding to inspection judgements (OFSTED 1995d). It is not clear, however, whether these projects will be undertaken by OFSTED itself or an independent body.

A number of important questions still remain unanswered. For example, is there confusion over what is the function of OFSTED and can the twin aims of inspection for public accountability and school development sit comfortably side by side? Can or should the inspection process move from being primarily about 'quality control' towards a greater focus on 'quality assurance'? Do OFSTED inspections lead to common practice and reduce diversity? Are they encouraging new forms of school management and governance, and if so, what are the implications of these for school development? Does the inspection give heads (and others) the necessary excuse or impetus to commence implementation? Is it merely a catalyst or a 'prompt' and under what conditions is inspection sufficient in itself to promote improvement? Can the developmental impact of the process be realised without effective school management? What are the various ways in which the inspection process can become 'owned' by the schools in order to promote improvement and encourage reflection? By what means might the detailed knowledge acquired by the inspection team be better used by the school for development purposes? How might feedback be best utilised? Is consultancy by inspectors following inspection commonplace and how valuable is it proving to be?

All of the above questions are largely unanswered but will need answering if we are to understand fully OFSTED's role and potential in school improvement. Clearly, these and many other issues are in need of further research.

CHAPTER THREE

Moving Together: a Partnership Approach to Improvement

by Louise Stoll and Maureen Thomson[1]

These days, everybody seems to have something to say about school improvement. To use an ice cream metaphor, it is definitely 'flavour of the month'. Agreement, however, is not universal on what motivates schools to improve. Some people believe that schools will improve in response to a variety of external accountability measures. For example, the Secretary of State described four pillars of improvement at an address to The Industrial Society (DFE 1995a): the National Curriculum, associated assessment and testing, performance tables and the inspection system with published reports. Many others, including those who have studied improvement efforts in Britain and elsewhere over the last 20 years, maintain that improvement comes from within and that those outside the school cannot mandate effective practice (McLaughlin 1990).

Doors to improvement

Bruce Joyce (1991) described different doors educators choose to open as they pursue improvement. We have updated his list to include doors currently being opened by educators in British schools. The recent surge of school-based interest in school improvement has developed, to a large extent, as a response to changes that have faced schools since the 1988 Education Reform Act. As schools have surfaced from underneath the externally imposed changes, they have realised that they still have an important agenda of their own that focuses on empowerment rather than control and self accountability. These doors to improvement include:

---

[1]With thanks to John Harrington and Dorothy Brown for their contribution to an earlier paper in which some of these ideas were first discussed.

- *Collegiality* – development of collaborative, professional relationships, through joint projects, team planning and problem solving.
- *Research* – study and use of research findings on school and classroom effectiveness and school improvement, through reading and discussion, course attendance and feedback to colleagues, or input from invited 'experts'.
- *Self-evaluation* – collection and analysis of school and pupil data, action research in classrooms and self-generated appraisal. While examination and Key Stage assessment data are mandatory, many schools choose to look at various academic and social development indicators and disaggregate results for different pupil groups, for example differences between girls and boys. Lack of progress or evidence of inequity signal improvement needs. Several Local Education Authorities provide schools with assessment information adjusted to take account of prior attainment, background factors or both. This enables schools to see to what extent they have boosted progress of their pupils. Teachers may also carry out their own focused classroom research, out of which improvement areas emerge.
- *Curriculum* – introduction of self-chosen curricular or cross-curricular changes or projects, for example reading initiatives or introduction of different kinds of IT.
- *Teaching and learning* – study of teaching skills and strategies, through discussion and staff development strategies. Examples include flexible learning and co-operative group learning initiatives.
- *Quality approaches* – emanating from business and industry – approaches, many of which can be submitted for external accreditation, include Total Quality Management (TQM) and 'Investors in People' (IiP).
- *Teacher appraisal* – although externally introduced, this is used by many schools to promote teachers' personal and professional development, with the aim of contributing to school development.
- *School development planning* – involving an audit of needs; decisions about priorities; construction of plans including responsibilities, timelines, staff development needs, required resources and success criteria; implementation activities; and monitoring and evaluation strategies. This approach offers the opportunity of opening all doors simultaneously.

Joyce argues that adherence to one internal approach alone is inadequate, and that major school improvement efforts need to open all the doors. Opening any of these doors, however, without attention to the deeper culture and organisational conditions of the school is unlikely to lead to improvement.

Partnership for improvement

Another door that can be opened is the partnerships door:

● Partnerships – voluntary activities and projects that link schools with one or more external partners in joint pursuit of improvement. Interestingly, external incentives for increased competition between schools have largely been resisted in favour of networking and clustering opportunities, as schools search for ways to increase collaboration between colleagues within school and beyond with other partners, towards the goal of improved effectiveness.

A report commissioned by OFSTED found 60 urban school improvement projects around England (Barber et al. 1995). These projects vary in their approach, and open *different* doors. Some have a specific curriculum focus. Others originate with data collection and analysis. Others are business Compacts, community education ventures or parental involvement schemes. What they have in common is that all use partnership as an improvement mechanism. Many have also been generated by LEAs in their new role since the 1988 Education Reform Act.

Several North American studies have demonstrated the importance of external school district support to successful school change (Rosenholtz 1989; Coleman and LaRocque 1990; Stoll and Fink 1994). There are strong arguments that the school cannot 'go it alone' and needs connections with outside agencies. Michael Fullan (1993) views the seeking of outside help as a sign of a school's vitality: 'It is the organizations that act self-sufficient that are going nowhere' (p86).

Essentially the school should neither see itself, nor be viewed, as an island. It needs to be the centre of change, and its success depends to a significant extent on its interactions with its environment. Over the years, many schools have built productive relationships with various partners. Nancy Watson and Michael Fullan (1992), commenting on The Learning Consortium in Canada, a partnership between four school districts and their schools, the University of Toronto Faculty of Education and the Ontario Institute for Studies in Education, conclude that strong partnerships are not accidental and do not arise purely through good will or ad hoc projects. They require new structures, activities and rethinking of the way each institution operates as well as how they might work as part of a network. LEAs, for example, severely affected by the reduction in their powers, have had to carve for themselves new roles that emphasise not only leadership but also willingness and ability to work with schools and other partners, 'losing an empire, finding a role' (Audit Commission 1989). Some have been more successful than others.

In this chapter, we examine one partnership between an LEA, its schools and a higher education institution This partnership, initiated by the LEA, is driven by the principle of school improvement from within but recognises external support and advice can assist the process. First we describe Lewisham LEA and its changing role since the Education Reform Act. We then explore the partnership between Lewisham, its schools and the Institute of Education at London University, embodied in the Lewisham School Improvement Project. The story of one primary school illustrates partnership in action. We conclude with key elements of partnership approaches to improvement.

Lewisham Education – a changing role

Lewisham LEA in South East London serves a diverse population, socially and ethnically, including areas of high deprivation. It took over responsibility for running an education service in 1990 following the dissolution of the Inner London Education Authority (ILEA). It serves 91 schools, of which 69 are primary, 13 secondary, 7 special and 2 nursery. The school population is 32,915 and languages spoken by the pupils number 126.

Since its inception Lewisham Education, like many other LEAs, has faced formidable challenges not least of which was the 1992 introduction of Local Management of Schools (LMS). The change in relationship between the LEA and its schools necessitated by the Education Reform Act formed the basis for reshaping the type and quality of services offered. It was the wish of both schools and the LEA to work together in a spirit of partnership that recognised the new responsibilities and roles and sought to develop, through co-operation, the best possible service for the education of Lewisham children. Joint working groups were set up between the Director of Education and head teachers, initially to plan for the new service and now to review and evaluate its effectiveness. These groups cover policy, planning, INSET, special educational needs, agencies and consultancies, and budget. Integral to the partnership is the desire to raise levels of achievement in schools and promote an improvement culture and language. The mission of the LEA encapsulates this:

> To lead and develop a comprehensive education service in partnership with the community to combat educational disadvantage and promote high levels of educational achievement for all.

Lewisham Education also recognises the importance of providing 'added value' to the work of its schools and takes seriously its responsibility for providing educational leadership. This responsibility is mainly with the inspectorate that was.

As schools became more used to local management they increasingly looked to the LEA as a supplier of services to enable them to carry out their own functions. The LEA, therefore, conducted some market research. From this it was clear that schools wanted a responsive advice and support service to meet *their* needs. In other words, they would request what they wanted, from whom they wanted, when they wanted. This information triggered the reorganisation of the inspectorate and advisory teacher teams into Lewisham's Quality Assurance and Development Service (QAD).

The Service consists of 30 advisers. The advisers work in partnership with schools to promote school improvement and effectiveness. Specifically, they work with schools and other LEA services to enhance pupil achievement through improvement strategies, assisted school self-review, professional, management and curriculum development. They also act on behalf of the Director to fulfil statutory responsibilities. QAD aims to support the development of self-regulation, to enable head teachers to take their schools ahead with confidence and power, and to help teachers, support staff, governors and parents develop as effective players in improving schools.

It is a widely held belief in Lewisham that schools do not change simply because advisers or inspectors go into them: they change by the talent and will of those within. An imminent OFSTED inspection might force a school to focus more sharply on its own performance, but it is the process of self-evaluation that is important. There is little evidence that inspection has generated subsequent improvement: it is merely an audit that tells you how things are, good or otherwise, and no follow-up advice is offered. In Lewisham it is considered that there is an alternative to inspection to raise educational standards. This alternative is to help schools make judgements on their own practice and performance, and plan with them ways to improve and measure their effectiveness. This can be achieved through 'critical friendship'.

Costa and Kallick (1993) describe a 'critical friend' as:

> ... a trusted person who asks provocative questions, provides data to be examined through another lens, and offers critique of a person's work as a friend. A critical friend takes the time to fully understand the context of the work presented and the outcomes that the person or group is working toward. The friend is an advocate for the success of that work (p50).

Schools need critical friends, individuals who, at appropriate times, listen and help them sort out their thinking and make sound decisions, who are not afraid to tell them when expectations for themselves and others are too low and when their actions do not match their intentions. They also help schools raise their expectations because critical friends care about schools and want the best for them.

In Lewisham QAD advisers aim to fulfil this role. They seek to understand the challenges and struggles facing schools at the moment, provide an objective viewpoint and knowledge of broader educational issues and try to help schools become more than they thought possible. Equally they have to gain the respect and trust of the head teachers and staff and establish a rapport related to responding, acting honestly, and protecting confidentiality when appropriate.

To assist their efforts in improving schools QAD, on behalf of the LEA, initiated a partnership with the Institute of Education. In the first instance advisers worked with the Institute to support head teachers and deputies to prepare their schools for the new and extended management responsibilities expected by LMS. All schools were required and supported to develop management plans within a common LEA planning framework. The title 'School Management Plan' (SMP) rather than 'development plan' was promoted to emphasise the need to maintain and sustain as well as develop (Hargreaves and Hopkins 1991).

Following the introduction of school management planning and the requirement of LMS for schools to be more accountable, it became necessary to know if schools were improving, how and to what effect. In seeking the answers, QAD were mindful of the need to find out more about the factors related to pupil progress and achievement and school effectiveness. They also saw it as important to be more analytical about the processes that lead to improvement. This led to the strengthening of the partnership with the Institute of Education through the development of the Lewisham School Improvement Project.

Lewisham School Improvement Project

The Project, which commenced in Spring 1993, has four aims that blend school effectiveness and school improvement goals:

- to enhance pupil progress, achievement and development;
- to develop schools' internal capacity to manage change and evaluate its impact at – whole school level; classroom level; pupil level;
- to develop the LEA's capacity to provide data to schools that will strengthen their ability to plan and evaluate change;
- to integrate the above with the system's ongoing staff development and support services to form a coherent approach to professional development.

The original plans and programme were supported by the Headteachers' Consultative, whose representatives joined Institute and LEA staff to form a management group. Day-to-day management and administration are undertaken by members of the QAD and LMS teams. At all stages and in all components of the Project, schools and individual teachers have volunteered to participate. By Easter 1995, more than three-quarters of the schools have chosen to be involved in one or more components. The five main components are:

1. Leadership development
2. School projects
3. Indicators creation
4. Evaluation
5. Dissemination.

Leadership development

Head teachers and deputy heads from primary, secondary and special schools attend a workshop series, 'Leaders Together' at which Institute and QAD staff help them to explore school effectiveness and school improvement research concepts. Workshops seek to enable school leaders to monitor and evaluate more rigorously the educational effectiveness of changes taking place in their schools, and develop coherent school improvement strategies that address issues of school culture, teaching and learning, management of change and staff development. Participants work in coaching pairs to solve school-based problems during and between sessions.

Reactions to this programme are very positive. In response to a follow-up evaluation, heads and deputies describe more involvement of staff in school management planning, developments in teacher observations, greater clarity in objectives and approaches to change, a sense of understanding about key school improvement issues, more constructive collaboration between heads and deputies, and an increased focus on learning for everyone in the school. One participant commented, 'Debate on the teacher as learner has been opened'.

School project

Ten schools bid to form a group of pilot schools. These schools (primary, secondary and special) are engaged in more intense work related to an identified teaching and learning improvement focus. Cross-role project teams attended sessions in which they worked with Institute and LEA facilitators to refine their focus through analysis of school-based data. They were also introduced to school effectiveness and school improvement research findings, with special emphasis on their change agent role within their schools. The workshop series title, 'Moving Together', reflected the impact on school improvement of teachers learning together

(Rosenholtz 1989). The teams continue to meet on an occasional basis. Evaluations of the workshop series demonstrated that participants believed their learning had been enhanced in various ways:

> 'It has made me read more, think more and have the confidence to relate information gained through and with others'.

> 'I am more prepared to speak, listen and become involved'.

> 'It has made me rethink my role in the school'.

Nine 'ground rules' have guided the work of these schools. These are based on findings of school effectiveness and school improvement research:

1. A focus on achievement in its broadest sense – to ensure that the central emphases are pupil outcomes, and teaching and learning. Examination of school effectiveness issues, including the notion of value-added (Goldstein and Thomas 1995) are included.
2. 'Start small, think big' (Fullan 1992b) – to ensure a manageable Project focus, linked to the school's management plan, in recognition that school development and classroom development go hand in hand.
3. Teams of people working together – reflecting the importance of shared leadership and teacher ownership.
4. Broad composition of teams – teams who co-ordinate the Project in their school and attend workshops represent the entire staff, and may also include other stakeholders.
5. Teams are agents of change – while the improvement teams are not responsible for change in their school, they need to facilitate that change, and therefore must understand the change process and its impact on people.
6. School management of the Project – because school improvement ultimately comes from within it is the school's responsibility to establish and maintain their Project focus, to manage the change process and to monitor and evaluate the Project.
7. Systematic monitoring and evaluation – the importance of setting success criteria, locating and dealing with problems, gathering and evaluating evidence, and using knowledge and information gained.
8. Support from outside – ongoing support is available from the LEA in the form of advisory services, present and tailor-made staff development programmes, resourcing, help with measuring indicators of achievement and development, and school visits. Support from the Institute focuses on strengthening the school's capacity to manage change effectively and reflect on practice, through accredited training and visits to individual schools. A critical friendship model guides all external support.

9. Dissemination to other schools – in the spirit of partnership, pilot schools share their findings with colleagues throughout the school system.

Improvement foci determined by individual schools include developing structured group work to improve individuals' achievement; raising achievement in non-fiction writing, underachievement of black boys, reading and specific curriculum areas. Strategies incorporate developing and testing new teaching and assessment techniques, teachers observing each other, use of teacher diaries, open meetings, invitations to external critical friends to provide feedback, student surveys, integration of school improvement plans into the school management plan, and in-service sessions run by school improvement teams for colleagues.

Indicators creation

A voluntary group of 15 teachers, head teachers, LEA advisers and officers have been working to identify and develop LEA and whole-school indicators of change, development and achievement. Against the background of the introduction of the government's Special Educational Needs Code of Practice (DFE 1994b), they have chosen to concentrate on pupils with special needs. They are developing indicators which will be available to schools when evaluating their effectiveness in respect of individual pupils' progress, whole-school systems and value for money. They provide data to inform the LEA's strategic planning, resourcing and monitoring roles.

Evaluation

Evaluation of change is fundamental to the Project and the question 'Has it made a difference?' a recurring theme. The intention has been for the Project to exemplify appropriate evaluation procedures and demonstrate effectiveness as well as encouraging and supporting schools to evaluate their own effectiveness.

The LEA collects Borough-wide data. It is used to inform school resourcing, compare the effectiveness of individual schools against LEA averages, study Borough trends in performance, track individual pupils, and provide baseline information for schools to use for evaluating their own effectiveness. The capacity for monitoring and evaluating effectiveness in primary and special schools is limited compared to secondary schools but pilot schools are being assisted to develop appropriate indicators.

The Halton Effective Schools teacher survey (Stoll 1992) has been adapted for completion by staff in the pilot schools and in a group of matched schools. It will be repeated after two years. The schools themselves also provide regular progress reports, addressing issues relating to success criteria, baseline data and progress to date. Initial progress reports were more concerned with school improvement processes than outcomes. Establishing teams and defining a school Project focus took some schools longer than might have been expected, but was important for developing understanding, collegiality and ownership. These reports recorded that involvement in the Project had positive impact on morale; led to improved communication reflected in more effective staff meetings, more focus on teaching and learning, and reflection. More recent Project reports demonstrate the increased emphasis on changing classroom practice and opportunities for student learning.

An Institute researcher is the evaluator of the Project. Through questionnaires and interviews, information has been gathered from school and LEA staff on their perspectives of individual school's progress.

Dissemination

Dissemination within and beyond the LEA takes place. The last two annual head teacher and deputy head conferences took school improvement as their theme, with pilot school heads, senior management teams and QAD members facilitating groups. Schools and LEA partners share experiences and understandings locally, nationally to other LEAs, at Institute of Education conferences and School Improvement Network meetings, national and international research conferences. A presentation to the International Congress for School Effectiveness and Improvement included all three Project partners: the Institute, the LEA and the schools.

The themes of improvement from within, self-evaluation and partnership are illustrated in the following description of the progress of one primary school.

Forster Park Primary – one school's story

The school has 370 children on roll and is situated in the middle of a large council estate. The area has high levels of social and financial deprivation and serves a working class community which is 70 per cent white and 30 per cent black and ethnic minorities. The local community is generally inward looking, often racist, and has low esteem and ambition. When the head teacher was appointed six years ago academic standards were low, behaviour and discipline poor and staff morale low. The school was perceived as unsuccessful by the LEA and the local community.

Over the years the staff and school community did an enormous amount of work on behaviour, pastoral work and management structures. This created a change of ethos, the achievement of which was reflected in a collegial feeling of mutual support and pride, but standards of pupil achievement were still unsatisfactory. Staff and parents did not have high expectations of themselves or the children in terms of achievement. Teachers saw themselves as 'coping with difficult children in a difficult community'. The head teacher felt that they needed to see themselves as 'teaching achieving children and impacting upon the community'.

At this time QAD started working in partnership with schools so the head teacher took advantage of available support and advice. She commissioned QAD advisers to assist her in a joint series of audits to evaluate the quality of learning and teaching and standards of achievement in the school. The aim of the audits was for advisers to work with the head, senior managers and governors systematically to: achieve full coverage of classroom activity and children's work within subject areas and across the school; evaluate teaching and learning quality and work standards by sharing evidence and reaching joint judgements; and summarise the judgements and discuss necessary interventions. Underpinning the whole process was the principle of leaving the head teacher empowered to move the school forward.

The audit findings provided necessary data to galvanise action. It made the head teacher more determined to raise educational standards. Her aim for greater effectiveness coincided with the introduction of Lewisham's School Improvement Project. She explained:

> 'When the School Improvement Project was presented to Lewisham head teachers it seemed to be the ideal project, at the ideal time in our development. After the Leaders Together component (during which head teachers and deputies looked at their definitions of school effectiveness and the ways to them) the bid which the deputy and I wrote focused upon changing the culture of the school to include more open discussion and study of instruction by developing the concept of teacher as learner.'

The staff were not consulted until after the bid was written, which the head teacher reflected was not an ideal way to proceed, but which was necessary due to time constraints. She also felt it had the merits of making her vision of school improvement very clear. There was agreement among staff that they all wanted to be involved but that the Project needed to be a tool to achieve already identified aims within the school management plan rather than a separate project running alongside. The staff wanted to be sure that the Project would not be an additional task which would distract them from agreed priorities. In retrospect, the head teacher saw this as the most important decision they took and one that was crucial to the success of the Project.

As the school management plan focused on language development they decided initially to focus on 'teachers as learners' in relation to teaching language and set success criteria which included the following:

- a more effective system for the dissemination of teachers' knowledge;
- higher levels of attendance at courses by all staff;
- improvement in classroom techniques – a closer match of learning outcomes to those planned, leading to raised standards in improved reading scores and achievements within the National Curriculum attainment levels;
- improved communication, with parents' attendance at parents' evenings and curriculum meetings, as staff become more confident and explicit in their explanations of practice and belief; and
- improved objective feedback from advisers.

A training day involved discussing and defining effectiveness in terms of school, teacher, head teacher, pupil and classroom. A team of volunteers were selected to be responsible for the Project's implementation. It consisted of the deputy head, a member of the senior management team, a middle manager and a teacher without extra management responsibility. To equip them for their role as change agents they participated in the 'Moving Together' workshops.

Although the head had seen the development of teachers as learners as primarily dependent on INSET, backed up by an in-school focus on teachers' skills, the team reversed these priorities. They put teacher skills and knowledge as the key factor and saw external INSET as a back-up to this activity. They began by setting up a programme of teacher observations. They wanted a clear practical focus which would impact directly on the classroom. All teachers were, therefore, asked both to name a teaching activity which they would be happy to be observed by a colleague, and to request someone to model a teacher activity in which they felt less confident. The discussion of teaching skills and strategies that resulted had a significant impact on classroom practice.

Aware of the need to keep all staff involved, the team had open meetings to discuss progress and feedback information on their training courses. Children's work provided the focus at these meetings, in which standards of achievement were moderated against National Curriculum attainment targets.

Over 18 months there have been many developments in the school. These include:

- teacher involvement in external research projects on improving reading;
- scrutiny by staff of the role of the curriculum leader in improving chil-

dren's achievement;

- greater teacher involvement in planning and offering INSET on their curriculum area, to the extent that there are insufficient training sessions to meet demand;
- heightened interest in the area of teaching strategies, resulting in these forming the focus of next year's School Management Plan;
- a much higher profile for assessment of children's learning, with non-class based teachers timetabled to give classroom release specifically to enable class teachers to concentrate on children's learning;
- ideas from articles and books being brought in by teachers to read at staff meetings, and share and implement them in school; and
- reports from children that indicate greater clarity about what they are learning and why: as teachers become more aware of their own needs and difficulties as learners they are more aware of the learning process for children and the need to be explicit about expected outcomes of lessons.

The culture of the school has undoubtedly changed but cultures need feeding. The school improvement team are reluctant to continue as the key change agent group because they feel that all the staff need and want to own the Project. This is an issue to be resolved along with the need to increase the involvement of support staff and governors, organise the collection and analysis of data more systematically and regularly, maintain what is good, continue monitoring the process of improvement as well as the outcomes, and further involve pupils in the process.

In terms of children's achievement the profile of academic achievement has already been raised. Standards of literacy continue the upward curve already begun before the Project started. The performance of Key Stage 1 children compared to National Curriculum norms is improving. Scores in the London Reading Test taken by Year 6 pupils show a decrease in the number of Band 3 children, with no change in pupil intake factors. The quality and range of writing, as judged by internal measures, has also been enhanced. The focus on analysing data on children's achievement is far greater and has pointed the school towards a more specific and sharpened focus on teaching and learning.

Key elements of partnership

While it is still early to make any final judgements, our experience over the two years leads us to identify certain elements of partnership that support the improvement process:

- *Shared values and beliefs* – a key characteristic of both school effectiveness and school improvement, this has been exemplified in the development of a common language throughout Lewisham, illustrated in the strategic plan and mission statements of the LEA and QAD, and the language now used by schools as they describe their improvement efforts. The most recent group to join the partnership and 'learn the language' are school governors who have been invited to participate in a complementary improvement Project.

- *Collaborative negotiation and planning* – involvement is essential to commitment. This depends on an equal partnership, demonstrated by school input and involvement in the Director's working groups, the market research exercise, and the design of the School Improvement Project.
- *Support* – support for schools is another vital ingredient of school improvement. The Leaders and Moving Together programmes and all other QAD INSET offerings have been tailored to support schools through the initiation, implementation, institutionalisation and evaluation of their improvement efforts. Representatives from the pilot schools have also shared their experiences with colleagues within their schools and across the Borough. Networks have also developed between Project schools.
- *Joint evaluation* – monitoring and evaluation, important conditions of any improvement effort, are strengthened by the 'inside-out, outside-in' perspective. In this partnership, examples have included joint school audits; cross-role group work on indicators development, Institute and LEA help with creation of specific success criteria for Project schools and associated measurement strategies; and collaboratively developed evaluations of the Project.
- *Critical friendship* – while school improvement ultimately cannot be imposed, the presence of external, impartial eyes appears to sharpen schools' foci for change. Examples of this are visits by LEA and Institute partners to schools, posing challenging questions; schools playing the same role, acting as critical friends for each other during staff development sessions; Institute help to teachers in writing and presenting to academic audiences; Institute evaluations of aspects of the Project, fed back to QAD advisers and schools; and the two of us writing this chapter together!

Conclusion

It is argued that one of the difficulties of schools taking responsibility for their own improvement is insufficient rigour in self-evaluation. The external inspection process is, to a large extent, based on such a premise.

There is, however, an alternative. Through a partnership approach, the empowerment necessary for real commitment to change, improvement and rigour can occur. Within such a system, inspection or external audits can become powerful and useful outside lenses to enhance improvement efforts.

CHAPTER FOUR

Improving Secondary Schools through Organisational Development

by Keith Pocklington and Dick Weindling

In this chapter we report progress to date on two school improvement projects which attempt to use an approach based on organisation development (OD). The authors are working as external consultants to support five secondary schools in two LEAs. OFSTED has the motto, 'Improvement through Inspection'; but we believe that improvement through this model is difficult as inspection has been separated from advice. Schools are therefore left to their own devices after the inspection has taken place to attempt to bring about any school improvement. We argue that the alternative model outlined in this chapter has much to recommend it. In our view school improvement must come from within, with outside support from consultants and the LEA.

School improvement in the UK

In the USA a large number of school improvement projects were begun in the 1980s. Most of these were based on the findings from studies of school effectiveness. Perhaps surprisingly, in the United Kingdom, improvement programmes have not been heavily influenced by the school effectiveness research. However, there have been initiatives – among them the following – which may be seen as attempts at various forms of school improvement:

GRIDS (Guidelines for Review and Internal Development) – (McMahon et al. 1984)
IBIS (Inspectors Based In Schools) – (Hargreaves 1984)
TVEI (Technical and Vocational Education Initiative) – (Employment Department 1982 to the present)

School Development Plans – (Hargreaves and Hopkins 1990).

Until very recently the term 'school improvement' was hardly employed in this country, but now a number of new projects have begun which are quite explicit about school improvement as their focus. Barber and colleagues (1995), on behalf of OFSTED, investigated the prevalence of 'urban education initiatives' in England, by which was meant 'any concerted effort by an organisation external to a school ... aimed at assisting the school to improve its performance'. Their survey – which depended on practitioners providing details of schemes in which they were involved – uncovered 60 initiatives varying in size, nature and scope. It is known that although comprehensive, this survey is not all-embracing, and that there is an even greater number of initiatives currently operating.

In order to give an indication of the variation in approach taken, brief details of some of these projects are given below.

One of the most established projects is that of 'Improving the Quality of Education for All' (IQEA), (Hopkins, Ainscow and West 1994). A team from the University of Cambridge Institute of Education are working with several LEAs and some 30 schools in East Anglia, London and Yorkshire. The overall aim of the Project is 'to strengthen the school's ability to provide quality education for all its pupils by building on existing good practice'. The emphasis is on collaboration between school staff and the external consultants. Schools contract into the programme, and in doing so accept a set of values for school improvement which have been developed at the Cambridge Institute. Each school designates a minimum of two people (one of whom is the head or a deputy) as project co-ordinators who attend ten days of training and support meetings. The group of co-ordinators form a 'project cadre'. Various staff development activities are undertaken by the schools and participating teachers are released from teaching in order to participate in the classroom-based aspects of the Project.

In Hammersmith and Fulham, a pilot project, 'Schools Make A Difference' (SMAD), ran between January 1993 and December 1994. It was LEA-led and involved all eight secondary schools in the borough. The Project had a number of broad defining characteristics which were drawn from the research literature on school effectiveness. It had as its main aim 'to lay the foundations for raising student levels of attainment, achievement and morale'. The schools were allocated money for physical modifications to the learning environment, and to support a range of educational provision and curriculum initiatives, e.g. revision centres and enrichment classes, literacy schemes, the adoption of active learning approaches, student monitoring and support schemes. Each school was required to put together a project bid for funding for the various developments specified, by means of which it was intended that improvement would be brought about. In an approach not dissimilar to that of the IQEA Project, there were regular opportunities for enhancing professional development, e.g. INSET sessions on a variety of topics and visits to schools beyond the borough to see examples of interesting and unusual practice. (For further details see Myers 1995.)

Staff from the London Institute of Education are working with LEA and school staff on improvement projects in the boroughs of Haringey and Lewisham (see Chapter 3). Personnel from the Centre for Successful Schools at the University of Keele are supporting similar projects in Shropshire and Staffordshire ('The Two Towns Project'). In addition, there is a funded Project on school improvement and raising achievement at the University of Bath, whilst the Manchester Metropolitan University is involved with a consortium of LEAs in the North West which are addressing the issue of effectiveness in urban schools. The Regional Staff College in Dudley is piloting a project which explores the application of the Deming approach to Total Quality Management in schools (see Chapter 6). Other LEA-based projects, some in collaboration with an HE institution, are currently taking place in Birmingham, Sheffield, Knowsley and Dorset. In addition to the studies mentioned, a number of individual schools have begun their own school improvement projects.

The CREATE approach which is described in this chapter, while it has some of the characteristics of these initiatives, is more like the school improvement projects mounted in the USA, and employs a process derived from organisation development. In order to understand the basis of our approach it is necessary to examine briefly the evolution of organisation development.

A brief history of Organisation Development

In their classic study, French and Bell (1984) see Organisation Development as a senior management-supported, long-range effort to improve the problem-solving capacity of an organisation, through an analysis of the organisational culture. Typically, this is carried out with the assistance of an external consultant using action research techniques.

A number of strands have led to the current conception of OD. The two most important names in this field are Kurt Lewin and Rensis Likert. After his arrival from Germany, in 1945 Lewin established the Research Centre for Group Dynamics at the Massachusetts Institute of Technology. He had coined the term 'group dynamics', and his work on the change process and action research were to have a profound influence on the staff associated with the various strands which came to comprise the field of OD. During a Summer workshop in 1946, he and his colleagues found that providing feedback, based on observations of community leaders working in groups, produced greater insight and learning than did lectures or seminars. From this experience emerged the National Training Laboratory in Group Development, where participants worked in groups supported by a facilitator and an observer. The use of Training Groups, or 'T-Groups', as this technique was later called, became one of the key strategies in OD.

Lewin also developed the notion of 'action research', which became the basic approach underlying most OD activities. Lewin and his co-workers employed the method on a variety of projects in the mid-1940s and early 1950s. As Lewin conceived it, action research comprised three main phases:

● Data collection
● Feedback
● Action Planning.

Thus, the link between 'action' and 'research' consisted of actions based on diagnostic research. The underlying belief was that action plans, designed to solve real problems, should be based on valid data generated collaboratively by the 'clients' and the consultants. Later, various modifications were made. Thus for example, Corey (1953) declared: 'Action research in education is research undertaken by practitioners in order that they may improve their practices'. This is the conception of action research used by many educationists in the UK today (see for example, McNiff 1988).

The second strand in the development of OD had its origins in the work of Likert, who established the Survey Research Center at the University of Michigan in 1946. Lewin and Likert knew each other quite well, and after Lewin's untimely death in 1947, most of his colleagues moved from MIT to Michigan, where in 1948 Likert became the Director of the Institute of Social Research. In that year Likert and Floyd Mann conducted a study of employee perceptions and attitudes at the Edison Company in Detroit. They discovered that substantial change occurred when managers discussed the survey results with their teams. This led to the development and adoption of the 'survey–feedback' method which became an important element in the OD approach.

As OD has evolved, its application has usually involved three groups of participants:

1. External change agents acting as consultants.
2. The client/client group – such as the senior management – seeking to enact some form of organisational change.

3. Internal change agents – a person or group inside the organisation to whom management has delegated responsibility for implementing change.

The hallmarks of the typical OD action research model are:

- collaboration among the three groups through a preliminary discussion of the problem;
- diagnostic data gathering by means of survey and interview;
- data analysis and synthesis;
- feedback to the client group and the people who provided the data;
- action planning and implementation.

The CREATE approach to developing effective schools

The origins of this work lay in the 'Effective Management in Schools' Project (Bolam, et al. 1993), together with our interest in the burgeoning literature on school effectiveness, school improvement, and the management of change. For a considerable time we had felt that some form of external intervention had much to commend it in terms of enhancing a school's current functioning. We believed that any school could improve, although they start from different points, and we were not thinking purely or even necessarily in terms of working with schools which might be described as 'struggling' or as experiencing serious problems.

Opportunities arose to work in this capacity with five secondary schools in two London boroughs in the Summer of 1993. Following exploratory talks with the TVEI co-ordinators and LEA officers, we outlined plans for an experimental, two year programme involving a small number of schools. We envisaged working in collaboration with teachers at each of the schools and with the appropriate LEA staff, notably the TVEI co-ordinator and other advisory teachers. We stressed that the precise nature of the Project in any given school could not be specified beforehand, since it would be formulated on the basis of discussion with the head and senior managers, interviews with a cross-selection of staff, and from having all teachers complete a diagnostic questionnaire which would capture staff perceptions of a wide range of features of school policy and practice. The anticipated outcomes for the programme would be: healthier and more dynamic school organisations; improved teacher practice, and hence better quality educational provision; which in turn should lead to raised levels of student achievement, motivation and behaviour over the medium to longer term.

The go-ahead for the Projects – described in more detail below – was duly given in each Authority. There were however crucial differences in the way that the Project was set up and implemented between the two LEAs. In one, following a proposal written jointly by the consultants and the TVEI co-ordinator, authorisation for a 12 month scheme in the first instance was received. We were directed by LEA officers toward two secondary schools which the Authority believed might benefit from the stimulus of external support. One of the two heads responded very positively to this opportunity, and a series of meetings were held with the head, members of the school's senior management, and ultimately the whole staff. However, the head of the second school did not respond with the same degree of interest, and after several attempts to open a dialogue, the consultants decided not to take the matter further. Several months later, the LEA proposed a replacement school, with which contact was made and we began anew the process of negotiating entry.

In the second LEA, the initiative began in a very different manner. Once again the consultants worked with the TVEI co-ordinator and put together a joint submission for funding a two year collaborative venture in three secondary schools. Four things about this scheme mark it out as different from that outlined above. First, there was more resourcing – partly because funding was secured from three sources rather than the LEA alone: the LEA (via the TVE budget); the Woolwich Building Society; and the local Training and Enterprise Council. Secondly, the heads of all secondary schools in the borough were invited to submit bids to take part. Each was required to make a case for why they wanted their school to be involved and what they hoped to derive from the scheme. Bids were subsequently received from six of the schools, and were considered by a selection panel. (The consultants were not represented on this.) Three schools were chosen to participate in the scheme. Thirdly, the involvement of the TEC brought with it encouragement for the schools to take part in 'Investors in People', a government-sponsored programme for stimulating investment in human resource development (see Chapters 8, 9 and 10 for further details). However, this was not a compulsory element of the scheme, and in the event only one of the schools opted to enrol at this stage. While expressions of interest were received from the two other schools, both decided to defer the possibility of entry to the 'Investors' scheme until a later date. Fourthly, a steering committee with widespread representation involving all the main stakeholders was convened, the purpose of which was to exercise strategic oversight and to receive reports of progress.

The school improvement process

Based on previous work, knowledge of the research literature and our understanding of the OD approach, we devised a strategy for school improvement involving a sequence of four broad but overlapping phases:

1. Entry and start up
2. School review and needs assessment
3. Planning and implementation
4. Monitoring, review and evaluation.

Each of the stages in the process is outlined below.

1 Entry and start up

This operated on two levels: the LEA and the individual school. With the former, discussion tended to be broad, covering the outline of the programme and the hoped for benefits. At school level it comprised preliminary talks with the head teacher, senior managers (and in some schools the governors) about how they saw the school's current state of development and the priorities for the future, together with a presentation to the whole staff on general ways of enhancing school effectiveness.

2 School review and needs assessment

Heads and senior colleagues were given the option of an organisational audit, whereby all teaching staff are asked to complete a diagnostic questionnaire which provides a detailed picture of school policy and practice. All five head teachers agreed that this should form the main starting point.

The diagnostic questionnaire The instrument was formulated as part of the DFE 'Effective Management in Schools' Project mentioned earlier, on which the two authors worked. As the title suggests, the major thrust was school management, which of course only forms part – albeit an important part – of school improvement. Accordingly, some modification was made to take account of the changed context, largely by introducing items which focused on the curriculum, teaching and learning and assessment.

Briefly, the CREATE instrument comprises a total of 89 items divided into seven sections:

School Ethos, Aims and Policy; Leadership and Management; Decision Making and Communication; Parents and Governors; Professional Working Relationships; The Curriculum, Teaching and Learning; and Managing Change.

Teachers are asked to respond to each item in accordance with a five point Likert Scale, where 5 equates to strong agreement with the statement and 1 signifies strong disagreement. The aim is to provide a snapshot in time of the strengths and weaknesses of the school as perceived by all members of the staff.

Examples of typical items from each of the sections are given below.

- *Ethos*

In this school:
- most teachers have high expectations of student behaviour
- there is a relaxed but purposeful working atmosphere for students.

- *Leadership*

The head teacher:
- has a clear vision for the future development of the school
- has his/her finger on the pulse of the school.

The headteacher and senior management team:
- work well together as a team
- command the respect and the support of most staff.

- *Decision Making and Communication*

In this school:
- staff generally feel that they are consulted on major issues
- teachers generally feel well-informed.

- *Parents and Governors*

In this school:
- parents are made to feel welcome
- many of the governors spend time in school and are known to staff.

- *Professional Working Relations*

In this school, teachers:
- feel able to express their views openly and honestly
- regularly discuss teaching methods and approaches in some detail.

- *The Curriculum, Teaching and Learning*

In this school:
- a strong emphasis is placed on high quality teaching and student learning.

In my department:
- the majority of lessons are challenging and absorbing for students.

- *Managing Change*

In this school:
- most innovation and change has been successfully managed
- a good balance is struck between innovating and consolidating.

Teachers complete the questionnaire in confidence. The consultants take away the completed forms for analysis, on the basis of which they prepare a written report, and a copy is given to every member of staff. This is normally followed up with a verbal presentation to all staff, who have the opportunity to question and comment.

In addition, each senior management team is given the further option of the consultants conducting interviews with a cross-section of the staff, to augment the information and insights derived from the diagnostic survey. This option was taken up in three of the five schools. The consultants helped to identify a cross-section of the staff based on a 25 per cent sample (approximately). Individual interviews were conducted with these teachers and senior managers (and in one school, some of the governors). The findings from the diagnostic questionnaire and the interviews provide a detailed portrayal of the school's climate and culture, and are used to devise the implementation strategy.

The possibility of surveying the views and opinions of students and parents – either through interview or by means of a questionnaire – was also raised by the consultants. However, to date neither element has been pursued in any of the five schools.

3 Planning and implementation

On the basis of the information obtained from the staff, together with the requirements of the head and senior management team, the consultants then drew up an implementation strategy. This outlined which aspects of practice needed to be worked on and how, who is to be involved and in what capacity, and any necessary materials and resources. How precisely things are taken forward will be unique to each school and will take account of the particular context and culture. However, the process may well commence with some form of vision building exercise which enables all staff and governors to map out the potential and realisable future development of the school over the next two to four years. There is also likely to be a range of presentations of relevant research findings as well as staff development of various kinds. Also, a co-ordinator may be identified or a small working party convened to inform and guide the evolution of the initiative in each school.

4 Monitoring, review and evaluation

This involves the gathering of formative data, which are used to inform and shape the process of development. It is important to stress that this element extends throughout the process of school improvement and is not a late add-on. In addition, a variety of information is collected for summative evaluation. One of the systematic methods is to repeat the CREATE questionnaire and examine any changes in staff perceptions. In the longer term, improvement on a number of student success criteria, such as attendance rates, test scores, attitudes, etc. are also needed.

Diagnosing the school climate

As we noted above, the diagnostic questionnaire was used in all five secondary schools, and has formed the starting point for our work in each school. On the basis of the five schools, what can be said about the commonalities and differences between them? Below we outline some of the more notable findings under each of the headings of the questionnaire. We would however stress that this is not an exhaustive comparison.

School Ethos, Aims and Policies Only in three of the schools was there a majority view that most colleagues were perceived to hold high expectations of student achievement. Only in two of the schools was the majority view that there was a relaxed but purposeful atmosphere in school. Hardly surprising then that in four of the five schools the majority view among the teaching staff was that most students currently were failing to realise their academic potential.

Leadership and Management All five head teachers were respected and liked as individuals by the bulk of their staff. However, only one of the heads was very favourably portrayed with regard to their role as the leading professional. Although all but one of the heads were seen to make themselves accessible to staff, only two heads were felt to be approachable by a majority of the staff. Differences between the head teachers were also perceived in their receptiveness to other people's opinions, and in their ability to provide a clear sense of direction for the staff. A perceived weakness of the senior managers in all of the schools concerned their ability to think and plan strategically. The views of teachers were more varied with respect to whether or not the senior managers were seen as an effective team. In one school a majority of staff considered theirs to be an effective team, whereas in two other schools the staff view was just as emphatic that theirs was not an effective team. In the two remaining schools staff opinion was more evenly divided.

Decision Making and Communication The extent to which many staff perceived themselves to be disempowered was very striking. In four of the schools the impression overwhelmingly conveyed was that the staff felt that their views were not taken sufficiently into account by senior managers when making decisions about the future of the school. Time and again teachers indicated either that their views were not canvassed and/or taken sufficiently seriously. Furthermore, substantial numbers of teachers in at least four of the schools felt ill-informed about developments affecting their school that were in the pipeline.

Parents and Governors In all of the schools the great majority of teachers believed that they worked hard to establish good relations with parents and to make parents feel welcome when on school premises. However, this did not appear to extend to involving parents in supporting and extending their children's educational development at any of the schools. Another striking feature was that the majority of teachers considered that governors had little influence on the day-to-day running of the school. In most of the schools staff believed that the governors were usually ready to follow the head's advice. In four of the schools the message was unambiguous: that for the great majority of the staff the governing body was a remote entity, with few opportunities for the contact necessary to develop mutual understanding and to build rapport.

Professional Working Relations Staff in all five schools conveyed the strong impression that generally sound working relations existed among the bulk of their colleagues. This included general advice giving and the sharing of good ideas, although it rarely extended to engaging in professional dialogue of a more substantive nature – for example, discussing what constitutes effective teaching and learning and possible ways of making this more effective. Furthermore, in at least four of the schools there was thought to be little in the way of inter-departmental collaboration, thus confirming the extent of 'balkanisation' across departments in secondary schools (Fullan and Hargreaves 1992).

The Curriculum, Teaching and Learning In all five schools there was a high level of agreement among the staff that, at least in their own department, the quality of teaching and learning was high – this in spite of the fact that, when asked in interview, teachers in four of the five schools could readily identify weaker departments in their school. In none of the schools were senior managers thought to spend sufficient time in the classroom observing lessons as part of monitoring the quality of teaching and learning. However, the impression we have is that teachers find it very easy to be critical of 'the management' yet find it hard to be critical of the quality of their own teaching and that of colleagues' classroom practice.

Managing Change In three of the five schools at least half the staff, and usually more, perceived that most change had been handled poorly. Only in one school did approaching 50 per cent of the staff indicate that change had been managed well. Further, in three of the schools a majority of staff felt that insufficient balance had been struck between innovating and consolidating.

What has actually happened?

After administering the diagnostic questionnaire, together with the programme of staff interviews in three of the schools, the outcomes were fed back to all staff. Subsequently, the consultants met with the head and senior management teams of each school to discuss these outcomes in greater detail, and to debate and agree priorities for moving into the implementation phase. In every case there was a need to identify priorities.

It is important to point out that we did not seek to impose our own agenda; it was seen as imperative to work with senior managers to shape an agenda with which both we and they were comfortable. Therefore, implementation in each school proceeded in different ways.

In this section we provide a brief description of what has happened in each of the five schools.

School 1

In the first school, although it was apparent that student underachievement and poor behaviour were seen to be real problems which staff faced, a difficulty of even greater magnitude appeared to be the poor relations between senior management and the rest of the staff. Many teachers felt disempowered, and they believed that their views and opinions were not taken into consideration. In addition, they lacked confidence in the ability of the senior management and of some middle managers to take the school forward. Systems of internal communications were ineffectual, which meant that details of developments which would affect staff did not systematically and routinely reach them. There was also felt to be harassment and even bullying of staff by some of those with greater formal authority. These and other factors were seen to have contributed to a climate in the school where staff felt unappreciated and undervalued. Lacking praise and support from senior colleagues, staff morale and motivation were low.

In such a setting, and in the absence of a clear lead from either the head or senior colleagues, the consultants felt strongly that attention initially should be directed at improving relations in the workplace. To this end we proposed that a planning group – the School Improvement Group (SIG) – be established to identify and agree the priorities and to devise strategies for improvement. In an effort to counter the decidedly top-down nature of planning and policy making in the school, the consultants pressed for the widest representation of staff (including support staff) on the SIG, and that decisions taken should be based on the principle of consensus. Both proposals were accepted by the head teacher and senior staff. The membership of the SIG included the head and deputies, the chair of governors and a cross-section of staff (teaching and non-teaching) who were elected by their peers as representatives for each level in the staffing structure. The consultants chaired each meeting of the group, and facilitated the group's deliberations by adopting the principle of consensus decision-making, whereby everyone present had to be able 'to live with the decisions and fully support them outside the meeting'.

We had envisaged the SIG membership fulfilling a dual function: feeding back to their colleagues accounts of the discussion and decisions, and feeding through to the SIG ideas, concerns and views from the staff whom they were representing. The SIG was seen as a means of opening up deliberations about future school policy and practice to a wider body of staff, and as helping to raise teacher morale and establish the notion of teamwork in a school that was characterised by disunity and division. It was also hoped that in the medium to longer term, members of the SIG might serve as focal points around which those of their colleagues keen to experiment with new ideas to improve teaching and learning might gather and find support.

In the event, the SIG duly provided a platform for more open discussion and served as a forum in which a number of promising ideas were generated. Sadly, however, few of the suggestions from staff were taken up by the head and senior staff and implemented. In retrospect, we realise that as consultants, we should have taken a stronger line to ensure that the head actively supported some of the proposals through the allocation of time and money.

School 2

In a second school in the same Authority, the outcomes of the staff interviews and the diagnostic exercise was to reinforce that here was a fairly successful inner-city school in which staff were pleased to teach. Any criticisms or shortcomings identified were very much subordinate to the school's strengths. The head was keen to strengthen the ability of middle managers to exercise management and leadership of their respective areas, and the consultants were asked to devise a programme of training and support. Prior to this one of the consultants led a vision building exercise as part of a whole staff development day. This proved both stimulating, productive and useful. Unfortunately however, before the training for middle managers could get underway, the Authority – concerned at the slow rate of progress being made, more especially in the first of the two schools – decided against providing any further funding and the initiative came to an abrupt end in both of the schools.

School 3

At this school, in the other LEA, following an extensive programme of staff interviews conducted by the consultants, a meeting of the whole staff – which the consultants facilitated – was employed as a means of debating the outcomes of staff consultation and identifying ways of addressing some of the more pressing problems. Further discussion with members of senior management took place and three main priorities subsequently were agreed: the SMT and communication; training for middle managers; and effective teaching and learning. At the time of writing, work has yet to commence on these.

School 4

At this school the head and senior management team identified middle management training and support as a priority. It was felt that too often middle managers were looking to senior management to resolve difficulties concerning their staff, and were not pursuing sufficiently thoroughly ways of enhancing the quality of teaching and learning provided within their area of the school. Accordingly, group interviews with all the middle managers were used to identify their professional development needs. The consultants then ran three half day workshops which addressed many of the needs identified, e.g. leading teams, managing change, strategic planning and evaluation. The evaluation feedback showed that the workshops had proved very successful and invigorating for all concerned.

However, although the need for training for middle managers had been suggested by the diagnostic questionnaire, this exercise also alerted the consultants to other potential problems, e.g. there appeared to be something of a gap between senior managers on the one hand and the main body of the staff – including middle managers – on the other. Teachers at all levels wanted more support from senior staff, and there were indications that they felt that their ideas, views and concerns were not sufficiently heeded by senior management. Again internal communications appeared to be less effective than they ought to be. Subsequently, following further discussion with the head and senior colleagues, it was agreed that the next step would be for the consultants to run a one day workshop for the SMT, to examine the concerns raised by staff and develop strategies to enhance SMT support. This proved very successful and led to a decision to restructure completely the consultative and decision-making processes in the school.

School 5

A very different line of development has evolved in the fifth school. Here the head teacher took a particular interest from the beginning, and was instrumental in authorising the go-ahead for an idea suggested by the consultants that a proportion of the school's 1994 pupil intake should be exposed to a pilot learning programme. It was agreed with the SMT that one of the three Year 7 groups should be assigned carefully selected teachers in the core subjects of English, maths and science, where the emphasis would be on enhancing the nature and quality of the teaching and learning. This 'experimental programme' subsequently went ahead, with direct support from an advisory teacher using programmes of cognitive acceleration and thinking skills. At the time of writing we have suggested conducting a series of interviews with students and staff to find out their reactions to the pilot programme – specifically, whether and how the way in which teaching and learning is conducted in these particular lessons differs noticeably from the students' other lessons.

At the same time one of the consultants has been supporting the SMT by attending some of their meetings and advising on the implementation of the OFSTED Action Plan. In addition the consultant has been involved in a training capacity at two residential weekend conferences for senior and middle managers.

It is too early to report how successful the school improvement initiatives have been, as many have only just got under way. Indeed, one of the main lessons we have learnt to date about this work is just how slow progress of any kind can be. As the projects proceed it will be important to have evaluative data related to a number of levels, such as: the school organisation and processes; the perceptions of teachers, governors, parents and students; and ultimately, some measure of student outcomes.

What lessons have we learnt about implementing school improvement?

In this last section we reflect on some of the key messages that we have learned from our experience of school improvement in secondary schools.

Establishing a contract All parties concerned need to enter into an agreement as to what each can expect of the other. What are the respective roles and responsibilities? What will the consultants do, and what will the school staff and LEA personnel do? Although we discussed these issues with both LEA and school staff, there were instances where some misunderstandings occurred on both sides. The drawing up of a more formal agreement might have helped to avoid this problem.

Clarifying the role of the consultants In each of the schools we have had periodically to clarify our role. This has entailed stressing to teachers that we are not subject experts, and working with senior managers and other staff to show that our role involves more than just delivering 'staff training'. Our particular expertise offers a combination of facilitation, training, and the use of research-based knowledge.

Getting started, pacing and timing It seems to take a considerable amount of time and effort to get anything underway, even in schools which have volunteered to be involved and hence, presumably, are reasonably keen. Overall, it has taken much longer than we anticipated. Possibly teachers and consultants hold different views about the pacing and timing in moving from discussion to action phases. The simplest explanation is that most schools and teachers are working very close to their limits and therefore have little spare time. Time is the most precious resource for schools and lack of time is a very real problem for teachers in school improvement projects.

Logistical problems There are problems for external consultants in being able to 'lock into' already established, up and running school systems and schedules (e.g. many schools have already planned their five INSET days for a year ahead). We tended to find ourselves 'out of synch', and it has proved difficult to fit in.

Identifying possible areas to work on and specifying priorities Aspects of 'evolutionary planning' come into play in school improvement. Although it is important to be as clear as possible about the priorities chosen to work on, these may well change as the project unfolds. It is important to do a few things well; and above all, not to become over-extended. The ultimate focus must be that of raising student achievement. Aim for as practical a pay-off as possible, with the central business of schools (i.e. teaching and learning) to the fore. However, working conditions, or organisational factors for school improvement are likely to require attention as well.

Getting the programme of school improvement to 'take' What factors and structures can help this? For instance, is a co-ordinator or a cadre of staff inside the school necessary, together with active leadership from the head or one or more senior managers?

We believe that it is essential to have 'allies' or 'promoters' to champion change:

- from among the SMT; and
- within the staff, e.g. a co-ordinator or a working party.

This helps to ensure that the project remains high profile and to keep things going when the consultants are not around. In addition, active support and leadership from the senior management is essential. They too have got to work hard to build commitment, offer reassurance and support staff.

If a school improvement group is established it needs to be representative of the potential 'stakeholders' (e.g. all levels of staff, governors, students, parents). It is necessary to clarify the precise roles and responsibilities of all involved, and to establish the links with existing decision-making structures.

Balancing pressure and support How do you strike the right balance of pressure and support? To date, most of our work could be seen as 'support'. In retrospect, it would seem that schools and teachers need quite a strong push from the external consultants in order for things to happen. We have come to realise that we need to take the lead more forcefully and be prepared to intervene more strongly in some of the schools.

Attaining a 'critical mass' There is a need to attain a certain critical mass – which is very hard – after which developments will take on a dynamic of their own, e.g. interested teachers may gather a few individuals around them and start setting up mini-projects of their own. But achieving that breakthrough has proved problematic.

Building an understanding of the complexity of the change process There is often a prevalence of anxiety about change in schools; staff have had enough change and cannot take any more. Effecting change is rarely easy or straightforward, hence there is a need to anticipate possible problems, and to look for small incremental gains. Building ownership of change only occurs as the project evolves. It is necessary to consult widely and thereby foster a shared commitment to change.

The symbolic significance of realising early successes Experience suggests that it is best to opt for something where there is a reasonable chance of attaining success, or being seen to have made a difference. This helps to both boost staff confidence and establish the consultants' credibility. It gives teachers a sense of power, of being able to influence things and effect change.

Attending to school culture as well as school climate We distinguish between climate – the surface and more observable aspects of schools, and culture – the deeper levels of ritual, history and values. An understanding of both is necessary for successful school improvement as contextual factors can constrain or assist the process.

Establishing at the outset a means of monitoring progress It is necessary to decide from the beginning how to determine what difference or impact the programme has had. This entails identifying and agreeing a number of performance indicators and success criteria. In most school improvement projects evaluation has proved difficult, and ours was no exception.

The effects of internal events Improvement projects can suffer setbacks if key players leave. For instance, in one of the schools there was a change of head teacher, which meant that we had to re-establish links and alter priorities.

The effects of external events This was most notable. For example, the fallout from OFSTED (i.e. planning paralysis in the lead up to the

OFSTED inspection, and staff morale largely shattered afterwards), affected three of the five schools.

The obvious point here – though it is sometimes overlooked – is that schools do not exist in a vacuum. Also, the welter of external initiatives in recent years has left teachers suffering from innovation overload, and therefore they may be reluctant to become involved in a school improvement project, which could appear to be just another initiative to have to cope with.

Exiting stage left How and when do the external consultants bow out? What is the exit strategy? This is, of course, the issue of continuation, and it raises the complex question of how do you help the school to build the capacity for sustained improvement and become a 'learning organisation' (Sengé 1990)?

What about other schools in the LEA? How can schools which have not been involved directly in the Project benefit? This concerns the issue of 'spread'. In one of the LEAs there will be a report to the Secondary Heads Group to keep them informed, and a major conference is planned to disseminate the messages of the Project to all the secondary schools in the borough. Also, the final written report of the Project will convey the key findings of the initiative.

We hope that this account of our experiences, even though we are only part way through the Project, will help schools, LEAs and external consultants with the complex but fascinating issue of school improvement. We have outlined a particular approach to school improvement which is based on organisation development. Our experience from this initiative leads us to believe even more strongly that school improvement is best achieved by external facilitators working collaboratively with school and LEA staff. This approach stands in contrast to that of OFSTED, which relies on external inspection to identify the strengths and weakness of the school at a particular moment in time, but leaves it to the school authorities to remedy the shortcomings identified. We believe that not only is this unduly wearing and stressful, but it is less likely to bring about fundamental changes. A further danger with the OFSTED approach could be that the association is made, at least in the popular mind, between school improvement and schools deemed 'at risk'. This would be regrettable, for school improvement is a process from which all schools can benefit. However, the complexities are such that improvement work must be sustained over the medium to long term, say three to five years. There is no 'quick-fix', because school improvement is steady work. It is essential that school improvement is not treated as just another passing fad but is seen as a vital means of improving teaching and learning.

CHAPTER FIVE

School Effectiveness, School Improvement and Good Schools

by Janet Ouston

This book reviews a range of different approaches to developing better schools. In recent years two approaches have dominated thinking: school effectiveness and school improvement, and school inspection. The effectiveness of inspection in supporting school development has been discussed in several other chapters here and in Ouston, Fidler and Earley (1996a). This chapter reviews the potential of work in the field of 'school effectiveness and school improvement' to assist schools in providing better education for their pupils. It will argue that they have made a specific, but limited, contribution. What is needed now to take this work forward is the development of theoretical models of the processes that underpin schools as organisations. As Kurt Lewin is reputed to have said 'There is nothing as practical as a good theory'.

School effectiveness and school improvement

For the last 15 years 'school effectiveness and school improvement' has been the cornerstone of thinking about how schools might provide a better education for their pupils; indeed it now has a GEST category named after it (see Silver 1994 and Mortimore 1995 for reviews of these areas). This chapter will review the potential value of these ideas in helping practitioners think about, and achieve, better education.

Before exploring these areas in more detail it must be made clear no doubts are raised about the importance of providing excellent education for all children. The concern explored here is that the area of study called 'school effectiveness and school improvement' has only a limited contribution to make and that other, very different, approaches are needed. By being quite explicit about the limitations we can then begin to see what is needed and why. The chapter will, therefore, start by reviewing some of these issues.

Warm comfortable words?

The first problem with 'school effectiveness', and with 'school reform', 'school improvement' and so on, is that no one could possibly disagree with the idea. These are 'good' words, they present a commitment to good education for our children. How can they possibly be challenged? Let me give you an example from a North American context. An American visitor to London said that he had spent his whole working life in school reform. My comment (which surprised him) was that I thought that was probably a very worthwhile and interesting life, but what exactly did it mean? What had he actually been doing? He was puzzled, but not offended, by my question – the English are permitted to ask these strange questions of Americans! – but I don't yet have an answer. To him the statement is self-evident.

On this side of the Atlantic too we have such words, and here too they are almost unchallengeable and do not need definitions. It is assumed that everyone knows what they mean and that everyone's meaning is the same. But is this so? Or is our use of the terms often so vague as to be almost useless except in creating a warm reassuring feeling that we are doing something worthwhile? Teachers often say that 'they are involved in a school improvement programme' but when questioned they may know what they are trying to achieve, but they rarely know *how* it will be achieved except at a superficial level.

Vaill (1991) in his thought provoking book *Managing as a Performing Art* distinguishes between *cults*, which he says have 'the feeling from outside that one either buys the approach or one doesn't', and *fields of enquiry* where 'divergent views, expectations of further debate and development are the norms' (p64). Ideas we take so much for granted as 'good things' can acquire a cultish quality which makes them unchallengeable (Ouston 1993).

Background

Before moving on to examine the concept of school effectiveness its intellectual underpinnings will be reviewed. In the mid-1970s these early research projects were called 'studies of school differences', and indeed I contributed to one of these (Rutter et al. 1979, reprinted 1994). Using Vaill's definitions, these studies were fields of enquiry rather than cults. Looking back they were of key importance in changing how we thought about the role of schools in children's development.

Fifteen Thousand Hours was published in 1979 (Rutter et al. 1979, reprinted 1994) and it was widely believed at that time that family influences on children's attainment were so overwhelming that 'schools could not compensate for society' (Bernstein 1970). Our work did not demonstrate that they could, even though it was sometimes interpreted in that way. Children from disadvantaged families did less well than children from more advantaged homes, and they doubtless continue to do so for a wide variety of reasons.

Our major finding, and those of other researchers such as Reynolds (Reynolds, Jones and St Leger 1978), was that children with similar test scores at the age of ten could achieve very different exam results at the age of 16 depending on which school they attended. Some schools appeared to be more effective than others in promoting academic attainment. The implication for schools was that they had a role to play in their pupils' development – they could no longer hide behind the statement 'what can you expect from children like this?' I have no doubt that this was a very important contribution to the educational debate at that time. Achievement was no longer seen as determined by social or individual psychological factors, and the impact of institutional factors was stressed. A later study of primary schools replicated and extended these findings (Mortimore et al. 1988).

Problems of definition

One of the problems with the concept of school effectiveness is that defining it in the real world is not only a technical or scientific issue but an ethical one. Researchers can define terms as they wish provided they are explicit. But once a word gets very widely used in the real world it can gain many shades of meaning and be so widely used that it loses precision. This has happened with 'school effectiveness and school improvement': the meaning has become quite unclear and is used in very different ways by different people.

For most researchers the concept of effectiveness is always linked with the measurement of individual outcomes which are aggregated for all the pupils in the school to assess school effectiveness. Usually exam results and/or test scores are used. These are seen by some researchers as the most important outcomes of schooling. Others may argue that there are other more important outcomes, but there are so many of them and they cannot be easily measured so it is best to focus on these and regard them as indicators of other less tangible outcomes. Again, for researchers this is not a problem, but for those in schools it is central as the outcomes measures used relate directly to their own educational values and aims.

Taking another example: a recent publication called *Effective Management in Schools* (Bolam et al. 1993) demonstrates the way in which the word 'effectiveness' has lost its precise meaning. This is a perfectly valid study of what teachers *perceive* effective management to be. It does not, however, tell us whether the schools described by their staff as 'effectively managed' were actually effective schools in terms of their outcomes. It seems possible (even likely) that they may be, but on the other hand the teachers' perceptions of effective management may actually be of high morale rather than effective outcomes.

Does the vague use of language matter? At one level it does not. We all want schools to be as good as they can be for our children. But the vagueness does matter for two reasons.

First, the widespread use of the word 'effective' often adds a spurious scientific underpinning, suggesting that we have established what an effective school is in all contexts. This is not the case. What we have is several studies of schools which were under or overperforming on test measures and some descriptions of what overperforming schools might look like. These are likely to be quite context specific. As I argued in a previous article ' ... the features that emerged as typical of effective inner city comprehensive schools would not, I think, have been found in an identical study of suburban grammar schools in the same city at the same time' (Ouston 1993). Brown, Duffield and Riddell (1995) report that, in their study of Scottish schools, there are clear interactions between the features of effectiveness and the social characteristics of a school's community.

There have, however, been many claims that studies of effective schools show the same features regardless of culture or community served. But perhaps this is only the case if the use of terms is very broad. For example, most studies of effective schools report that leadership is of key importance. But this is a statement of the obvious – we would, I think, be very surprised if it was not, or if 'poor leadership' was associated with effectiveness. The problem with these very general statements is that they don't actually help us to go forward. They do not answer the reasonable question from a reasonable head: 'Well, what do I do on Monday morning in this school?' Once one considers the details of leadership style, what is appropriate for one school might be quite inappropriate for another.

In his report Her Majesty's Chief Inspector (OFSTED 1995d) makes a similar point. Referring to school effectiveness research he says:

> It may be however that we already know what we need in order to make a difference in the real world: effective schools are well run schools; where teaching is purposeful and the teachers' expectations of children high; where progress is monitored systematically; and where parents are involved in a

genuine partnership. Further research into such questions might prove useful, but the real questions are the practical ones concerning the improvement of the individual school.' (p9)

I, too, would stress the emphasis on the *individual* school and on the need to move on from rather vague lists of features of effective schools. School improvement will be discussed in more detail later, in particular the extent to which individuality has to be taken into account. In a paper reflecting on a curriculum innovation at her school, McHarg (1995) wrote: 'I would suggest that this approach to the management of change is not ideal but fitted these particular circumstances and this particular staff'. My view would be that if it did fit the people and the time, in that particular school, then it *was* ideal.

Effective for whom?

A second problem relates to this issue of what we mean by 'an effective outcome', or 'effectiveness for whom?' In his recent annual report Her Majesty's Chief Inspector of Schools (OFSTED 1995d) published the names of 52 schools that had 'received very positive inspection reports and achieved an improvement of around or greater than 10 per cent in their examination performance between 1992 and 1994' (p3). A subsequent analysis, however, pointed out that one-third of these schools 'have registered no improvement or a decline in the achievement of lower ability pupils' (Pyke 1995). I am not commenting on this example to argue for or against particular measures of effectiveness but just to point out that even if we agree on a definition of effectiveness (here, performance in GCSE exam results) questions of educational value still remain.

Do we measure attainment or progress?

The more the term 'effectiveness' enters the mainstream educational world, the more this technical issue gets ignored. Increasingly professionals in education (OFSTED inspectors, for example) are making statements that 'this is an effective school'. But there are two very different approaches to the measurement of effectiveness which will provide very different outcomes. One is the exams league table or the tables of National Curriculum assessment results. These include raw exam results or test scores which take no account of the previous attainments of children at the school. Thus, in these terms, a school with a favoured intake will almost inevitably appear to be 'more effective' than a school serving a disadvantaged area.

The original studies of school differences in the 1970s attempted to make statistical adjustments for differences in intake to assess the 'value added' by the school. Recently much more sophisticated methods such as multi-level modelling have been developed to do this (Goldstein 1987). The Department for Education has recently commissioned a study to develop a national approach to value added league tables.

Another way to take account of earlier attainment is to consider measures of progress. This approach was used in selecting the 52 effective schools listed in HMCI's Annual Report (OFSTED 1995d). There is, however, an additional problem with this approach in that schools that had sustained a high level of performance over two years would not have been identified as an effective school. A school that had an exceptionally high level of performance on the first occasion would not be able to 'improve by 10 per cent'. This very successful school could not be included in HMCI's list.

Do we need both types of measure?

Researchers have generally argued that value-added, or progress, measures are more valid indicators of school effectiveness than are raw measures such as we see in the school league tables each year. But this depends on what you want to use the measures for. For some purposes, selecting a school for a child, for example, parents might reasonably require both sets of information. They might understandably choose a school with high raw exam results, that was not underperforming in terms of its intake, against a school that had low raw results but was over-performing. Schools, too, might prefer to use raw measures to assess their own performance.

Are we justified in making fine distinctions in the performance of schools?

Recent work has undercut the early findings on differences between schools. Using more sophisticated analytic tools than were available in the 1970s, Goldstein and colleagues (1993) have demonstrated that it is very difficult to distinguish between the relative effectiveness of the majority of schools. A very small number can be identified as under or overperforming, but that there is no statistical justification for ranking the vast majority. To quote from Goldstein (1993):

> ... value added analyses yield uncertainty intervals which are so large that only schools with extremely small or extremely large value-added scores can be separated from the remainder. In other words, it is not technically possible with any reasonable certainty to give an unequivocal ranking of schools in a league table, whether this is an unadjusted raw table or an adjusted value-added one'. (p34)

Goldstein and colleagues (1993) also reported that their analyses of relative effectiveness produced different outcomes for different subjects.

The problem of variation

The presentation of schools that have 'made a 10 per cent improvement' may attempt to get over the problem of different intakes to schools but it raises a far more serious issue. Schools, in common with all other organisations, have variation in outcome from year to year. Schools with a lot of variation can be seen as unstable – and unstable organisations are very difficult to change. The schools with most variation are those that are likely to figure on the HMCI's list, but may well be the most difficult to improve consistently over a period of time. They may just be up one year and down the next. This is an important issue which will be explored in more detail below.

Moving from school differences to school effectiveness

Having established that schools differ from one another in their outcomes, either in terms of progress or attainment, the researchers then linked outcomes to aspects of school practice. Essentially what they were trying to do was to describe the key features of effective schools so that these could be introduced into less effective schools to improve their effectiveness and hence their students' outcomes. There are, however, some major problems with this approach which will be reviewed next.

School outcomes

If Goldstein is right in arguing that most schools cannot be distinguished from each other in terms of their outcomes, then it is potentially very misleading to use the resulting league tables of school outcomes to identify features of effective practice. All that could be distinguished are the differences between the most effective schools and the least effective at either end of the range of schools.

Cause and effect

It is almost impossible to unravel questions of cause and effect from this work. An extreme example will illustrate the point. In our early study (Rutter et al. 1979, reprinted 1994) we found that the more effective schools tended to have more pot plants in classrooms – pot plants in classrooms correlated highly with effectiveness. This example is deliberately chosen to make the point that the pot plants were probably a consequence of many other good things going on at the school rather than the cause. Place pot plants in a poor school and they would die! There may be many other features of effective schools which are the consequences of effectiveness rather than the cause.

Researchers' decisions

The lists of features of effective schools are, of course, directly a consequence of the researchers' decisions about what to collect information about. These decisions will depend on the researchers' own educational values and their implicit theories of the links between educational practice and educational outcome.

List logic

Barth (1986) argued strongly against 'list logic'. Yet this is exactly what comes out of studies of school effectiveness. The lists are never ordered or weighted in terms of importance, and they never include any understanding of the process of the organisation. It's like defining a cake in terms of its ingredients only. Of course we need to know what the ingredients are, but to make a good cake we also have to know about the general processes of baking.

Time lags

Effective schools are usually defined according to the progress made by pupils over a three to five year period. As an example, consider a child who entered secondary school in 1980 and took their GCSE examinations in 1986. This child would have been influenced by that school from 1980, but the value added analysis would be published in 1987 and conclusions drawn in 1988. Other schools start implementing those ideas in 1989 and 1990 nearly ten years after the research group entered secondary school. The time delay is huge and may make research quite irrelevant given how fast the educational context, and society's expectations, change.

Learning from effective schools

One of the implicit assumptions of school effectiveness research has been that lessons from studies of effectiveness can be applied directly by schools to lead to school improvement. The remainder of this chapter is concerned with whether this is a reasonable expectation. Reynolds (1995) argues that 'school effectiveness snake oil' cannot be applied to failing schools. This chapter extends Reynolds' thesis, arguing that studies of school effectiveness have very little to offer schools in general unless they are underpinned by an understanding of the *processes* of schools: of how particular processes lead to good or poor outcomes.

Interestingly, much of the school improvement work reported in the

1980s (e.g. van Velzen et al. 1985) developed almost independently. School improvement and school effectiveness were two different areas of study. But each was only descriptive, and school improvement studies too ended up with lists of 'key features of improvement'. Stoll and Mortimore (1995) summarise this research and link together the features of effective schools and the 'facilitating conditions' for school improvement.

While there may be some processes that are common across all schools, it seems likely that they will be different in different schools. Every school has its own history, staff, values, leadership, culture and so on. Each school has to improve itself in its own way. What is right for school A may be quite wrong for school B even though it may be located in the same area and serve a similar catchment area. Most improvement programmes are based around school development planning (Hargreaves and Hopkins 1994) but these do not offer a theory of how organisations work, nor how effective change might be achieved.

What do studies of school effectiveness have to offer?

To sum up, this body of research has drawn attention to differences between schools – some schools do seem to be more effective than others. But the assumption that schools can merely copy effective practices and improve themselves is probably very unlikely for all the practical and technical reasons set out above. Most school improvement programmes are based on school development planning (Hargreaves and Hopkins 1994) in some form, and have rarely moved to more detailed analysis of school processes and functioning.

The complexity of schools

Schools are such complex systems that one can never assume that one action will lead to one outcome – or even a set of possible outcomes. The reality is that the system is so complex that we can never achieve predictability; as a consequence there will never be a single recipe for achieving a successful school.

Brown, Duffield and Riddell (1995), and Reynolds (1995) discuss the particular issues concerning very ineffective schools. Schools in serious difficulties may not have a store of professional expertise distilled from experience that will help them to improve. In contrast, moderately effective schools have lots of experience and strengths to build on, and may not need any theoretical understanding to make adequate progress. This is not to say that they would not make more progress if they had 'a good theory'!

The complexity of schools as organisations also suggests that we have a choice of conceptual routes: either we develop more and more contingency theories where, for example, we attempt to identify particular strategies that lead to improvement in particular types of schools, or we develop theories that include differences between schools as a central part of the theory. This will lead to a more unified theory of the links between school practice and outcome for pupils but inevitably these theories will have to be at a higher order of generality. This issue is discussed by Heckscher (1995, p44). Hargreaves (1995b) is also concerned with developing overarching conceptual frameworks which link studies of school effectiveness with studies of school improvement. He explores the concept of school culture as a way of describing effective schools and recording the changes related to school improvement. These methods are proposed for researchers, to enable them to describe and record, rather than for practitioners who need a model for helping them to implement change.

Earlier in this chapter the list of outcomes of school effectiveness research was compared to a list of ingredients in a recipe. To extend this analogy further, three things are needed to bake a successful cake: a list of ingredients, the quantity of each ingredient and a method. School effectiveness research might be seen as providing us with the list of ingredients only. If a moderately experienced and successful cake maker was only given this list he or she could probably bake a reasonable cake drawing on previous experience and some experimentation. This might be seen as the position of moderately effective schools drawing on the results of school effectiveness research. They already have some skills needed to improve themselves.

A less effective school may be completely unable to become more effective without stronger conceptual frameworks: they may need either very detailed instructions to help them to bake a specific cake, or some understanding of the general principles of baking. Given the complexity of schools it seems likely that the 'very detailed recipe' will never be a successful approach to school improvement, but an approach focusing on higher order general principles may be very helpful. To return to baking: this approach will allow the baker to substitute ingredients, to tailor ingredients and methods to produce desired outcomes, and to understand failures. Why did that cake have a hole in the middle? In organisations, too, we need some general principles which can be applied to a whole range of organisational issues. The remainder of this chapter presents a brief introduction to one possible approach – that of Deming – which is explored in more detail in the next chapter by Hinkley and Seddon.

An alternative metaphor might be taken from medicine. First we need to describe the difference between illness and health – in what way is this person 'ill'? (This is the model of school effectiveness work.) Then we need to think about how the patient might be helped to become healthy. (The equivalent of school improvement.) An obvious first approach might be to observe the recovery of people with this condition, then try to recreate this changing pattern of symptoms using appropriate interventions (the school improvement model).

Let us assume that this patient has the 'flu with a headache, a raised temperature and quite severe depression. This first stage, of diagnosis, is of key importance but it does not (and can not) *by itself* lead to improvement. (Similarly, the audit phase of school development planning, and possibly inspection, are of importance, but they do not lead directly to improvement. Being told that the school has to improve on six 'key issues for action' will not lead to improvement. The problem with OFSTED's logo of 'Improvement through Inspection' is not that it's not possible, but that the simple word 'through' slides over so many different processes and concepts.) Returning to our 'flu-bound patient, we might offer painkillers and a cold bath to reduce the temperature. We are not quite sure what to do about the depression. Is it part of the illness, or a consequence of the illness? Similarly with school effectiveness – we can never distinguish between causes and consequences. Should we give this patient anti-depressants? This depends on our model of this illness.

Aspirin and cold flannels are likely to be effective with a patient who is young and generally robust: the combination of specific action, time and good general health will probably lead to recovery. (This could be seen as similar to the use of lists of 'facilitating conditions' in school improvement.) But we still do not have a theory of why this patient is ill, and without a theory our practice can never be more than the blind pulling together of experience. Going back to the analogy with medicine, we are at the folk medicine stage – what Reynolds (1995) was referring to as 'snake oil' perhaps – where we know from experience that certain herbs (or snake oil) are useful in certain illnesses but we do not know why they should be effective.

We could create many theories to explain the condition of this patient: virus theories, psychosomatic theories, even witchcraft. Each of these may have some place in helping the patient to improve, but they have the great advantage that they are generalisable to more than a single individual and they can be tested. By moving away from description towards an understanding of cause and effect we have established a new conceptual framework which can extend our understanding of illness. It is exactly this that is needed to take school improvement work forward.

In the revised *Handbook for the Inspection of Schools* (published in October 1995) the inspectors are required to prioritise the Key Issues for Action. This new requirement will begin to raise the issue of how schools function as organisations: what are the chains of cause and effect in this particular school? The implicit theories that inspectors hold will underpin their prioritising of the issues for action. Their theories may, or may not, match those of the school's senior managers, who in turn have similar, or different, understandings to the rest of the staff. Unless the processes of the school are understood, they cannot be changed.

Alternative conceptual approaches to improvement

There are, of course, many different approaches to understanding the processes of schools, just as there are many different theories of illness. Two contrasting approaches, for example, are those of 'organisational development' (OD) and of Deming's ideas of 'continual process improvement'. Each of these meets the requirements set out above. They attempt to understand the functioning of organisations, to understand why particular actions will lead to certain outcomes, and to offer new ways of thinking about organisational change. They both focus on organisational processes, and the causal relationships between processes, within a larger system. Both are illustrated in this book: Hinkley and Seddon's chapter uses Deming's ideas, while Pocklington and Weindling, and Zienau use concepts from OD.

Continual process development

The remainder of this chapter will explore Deming's ideas as one approach to creating organisational change which goes beyond merely describing changing organisations.

Deming is often remembered as a guru of Total Quality Management, but he denied that himself. His interest (Deming 1993) was in developing a theory about work organisations that would lead to improvements in what the organisation achieved. His approach is directly relevant to education, but sometimes difficult to grasp. The main problem is that in contrast to most writing in education, his theories are content-free – they focus almost entirely on process, on 'how' rather than 'what'. His ideas are not located within a particular type of organisation, but can be applied to many. He was concerned with common principles of people working together in order to achieve a common goal rather than specifically about schools or offices or manufacturing industries. His theory leaves the reader to fill in all the practicalities and to learn about the organisation and the theory in the process of using it. This process of learning is a key part of developing the theory to fit the specific organisation. Secondly, his work is not written in an 'education-friendly' style. It is the very concise writing of an engineer; the reader has to think hard about how the ideas might apply to the life of a real school. Finally, like many other American business gurus, the enthusiasts have created a cultish quality about his work that more reflective academics may find distasteful. But regardless of these reservations, it is argued here that these ideas may lead us to a very productive way of thinking about continuous improvement in schools. The key concepts are explained briefly below: the next chapter presents more details of their application in schools.

Appreciation for a system

All organisations are made up of interdependent systems. Understanding the system is of central importance for those managing them. If you don't understand a system then you cannot reliably change it. (Hitting the side of the television may keep it working for a while, but an understanding of television sets is needed if a real improvement is to be made.) Because the systems are interdependent, changing one part of the system will have consequences elsewhere – and these may be undesirable. 'Quick fixes' may lead to adverse outcomes.

A system is seen as consisting of processes (i.e. activities) and an aim or purpose. The aim may not be explicit, but all activities have some purpose for someone even if it is a low level aim (for example, keeping the children occupied and quiet). Systems can be perceived as existing at many different levels from the single classroom to the whole school. Understanding the links between classroom systems and school-wide systems is a complex issue, but it is one that school managers have implicit theories about to underpin management decisions. Similarly, teachers have implicit theories about the links between teaching and learning which guide their classroom practice. Making these processes and systems explicit, and testing them out, will provide the basis for improvement.

Within each system there are chains of internal customers and suppliers: the language is uncomfortable for educators but it can be helpful in understanding processes. Because of the interdependence of systems the effectiveness of these internal chains of customers and suppliers are quite critical to the effectiveness of outcomes. Consider the head teacher and the school finance officer as part of one chain. Sometimes the head is the customer of the finance officer and requires information from him or her; sometimes the roles reverse and the finance officer is the customer and the head the supplier. The school will only be effective when all these chains work well, and when the expectations of the various groups of customers are met.

One of the problems for schools is that they have many groups of customers, and their expectations may be in conflict. Teachers, parents, pupils, OFSTED, the National Curriculum and governors could all be seen as customers of the school. One of the arts of leadership may be to identify the common areas and decide how to resolve areas of disagreement. A related issue is that of seeking a balance between sub-systems. If sub-systems are encouraged to maximise their own performance this may have a negative impact on the outcome of the whole system. Individual departments pursuing their own concerns may not be in the best interests of the whole school. Similarly individual schools maximising their own performance may not maximise the performance of the whole education system. Difficult decisions may have to be taken in order to achieve the best outcome. These decisions are not value-free, but an analytic approach may help to clarify the issues.

Many of the implications of Deming's work are concerned with understanding and improving processes. First they are analysed, and then small improvements are made. These are reviewed and again improved. Process improvement becomes a regular part of the organisation's culture, and leads to each person (teachers and pupils) becoming in part responsible for the outcome of the whole.

Understanding variation in systems

No human system will operate the same way all the time. Outcomes will vary due to a wide range of causes. Most variation will be due to what Deming called 'general causes'. They will reflect the variation within the whole complex pattern of interlinked systems. It is this variation that is due to general causes that is particularly responsive to management actions. But sometimes particular outcomes will occur which are way outside the normal range. These are generally due to specific causes, and should be handled as one-off events. They may relate to the actions of individuals within the system rather than the system itself. One of the key arts for a manager is to be able to distinguish between variation that is the result of general causes, where management action on the system is the most effective, and variation which is due to specific causes where individual action is needed. In some aspects of school life it is possible to collect data to examine sources of variation (see for example, Greenwood and Gaunt 1994), but even if this is not possible an understanding of variation is critical. One of the aims of a manager is first to reduce variation so that the system is less unpredictable, then to introduce process improvements which lead to an upwards trend. The example presented earlier of schools that had improved their exam results by more than 10 per cent may be merely unstable rather than improved.

The danger for schools comes from confusing these two sources of variation. Variation due to general causes requires system-wide action (or no action), while specific cause variation may need a one-off localised response. In practical terms: a parent complains vigorously about a particular incident – are you going to treat this as a general issue, a specific issue or ignore it? And if you do decide to take action on the system, what impact will this have elsewhere? Deming warns against 'tampering' with systems – what elsewhere are called quick fixes, because if they are not analysed very carefully there may be system-wide consequences that are worse than the special event that provoked them. One of the implications of this approach is that often those with management responsibilities make too many decisions rather than thinking about and analysing the processes first.

Motivation

Deming argues that managers can never motivate staff, but demotivate them. He sees the responsibility of those in management roles being the reduction in demotivating factors within the organisation, thus allowing the intrinsic motivation of teachers and pupils to flower. He builds on psychological theories of motivation that point to the demotivating impact of target-setting, performance-related pay, etc. Feedback about performance in order to improve is a powerful motivator, but setting artificial targets and grading will demotivate and lead to distortion and 'cheating'.

Contribution of Deming's ideas to school improvement

These ideas are proving very powerful in a small pilot project currently being undertaken in schools in the Midlands. Hinkley and Seddon describe work in these schools in the next chapter; Greenwood and Gaunt (1994) present a critical review of the application of these ideas in schools. This chapter has reviewed the contribution that studies of school effectiveness might make to school improvement and has concluded that they are limited by the lack of an underpinning theory of how schools work. A brief review of Deming's ideas was then presented as a challenge to existing ways of thinking about the management of schools and classrooms.

CHAPTER SIX

The Deming Approach to School Improvement

by Tony Hinkley and Jane Seddon

'By what method?'

Sometimes we can still hear the unmistakable voice of Dr W. Edwards Deming booming out across the crowded lecture hall.

'By what method?'

It was a response he usually gave to statements made by some unsuspecting member of the audience at his seminars. This response was elicited especially when the delegate was attempting to describe how inspection of their product or service was going to bring about improvement. Deming was unequivocal in his response – inspection in itself never brings about improvement. Improvement comes from a systematic transformation in organisational culture, and not from end-of-process inspection. He gave the world a philosophy and a methodology to bring about such a transformation, and to achieve the seemingly impossible dream of 'joy in work' (including learning).

Deming's work emphasises the futility of end-of-process inspection to control quality of product. He advocated that improvement in quality of product (or service) involves the active participation of the whole workforce in the improvement of the processes in which they operate, and that managers and leaders need to develop their understanding of this dimension of their role. The responsibility of managers and leaders is to work on the system to improve it (with the help of those who work in the system), as opposed to setting arbitrary targets and measuring only the outcomes of a process.

During the later years of his life he committed to paper his philosophy firstly, in 1986, in his best known book, *Out of the Crisis*, and more recently, in 1993, months before he died in *The New Economics for Industry, Government, Education*. In his earlier work he described his '14 Points for Management' (Deming 1986, pp23–24) as the '... basis for transformation of American industry … '. Equally they apply to industry, health, education and government anywhere in the world, as his later work showed.

It is worth, at this juncture, to list these 14 points for management, and to add a summary of an interpretation of them for education. This has been produced by a school which has embraced Deming's philosophy to staggering effect (in improvement in achievements and confidence in its students). The headings are Deming's words, the italicised notes were produced by a class in Mt Edgcumbe High School, Alaska, in 1990.

---

1. Create constancy of purpose
Aim to create the best quality students capable of improving all forms of processes and entering into meaningful positions in society.

2. Adopt the new philosophy … take on leadership for change
Educational management … must learn their responsibilities …

3. Cease dependence on inspection to achieve quality
Eliminate the need for inspections on a mass basis … by providing learning experiences which create quality performance. Work to abolish grading and the harmful effects of rating on people.

4. End the practice of awarding business on the basis of price tag
Work with the educational institutions from which students come. Improve the relationships with student sources and help to improve the quality of students coming into your system.

5. Improve constantly … the system
… of student improvement and service, to improve quality and productivity.

6. Institute training on the job
… for students, teachers, classified staff (ancillaries) and administrators (managers).

7. Institute leadership
The aim of supervision should be to help people use machines, gadgets and materials to do a better job.

---

8. Drive out fear
... so that everyone may work effectively for the school system. Create an environment which encourages people to speak freely.

9. Break down barriers between departments
People ... (in every department) ... must work as a team.Develop the strategies for increasing the co-operation among groups and individual people.

10. Eliminate slogans, exhortations and targets
... asking for perfect performance and new levels of productivity. Exhortations create adversarial relationships...

11. Eliminate quotas, ... management by objective.
... (e.g. raise test scores by 10 per cent and lower drop outs by 15 per cent). Substitute leadership.

12. Remove barriers that rob ... of pride of workmanship
... for students, teachers and managers (including merit rating and performance related pay)

13. Institute ... a programme of education and self-improvement
... for everyone.

14. Put everybody ... to work to accomplish the transformation.
It is everybody's job.

Who could argue with these 14 points? Putting them into practice, however, requires brave and intelligent managers who are willing to learn. The 14 points should not be taken as a checklist or recipe for transformation – this is not Deming's legacy. The 14 points might be said to be the manifestations of the method, not the method itself. What is required is a deeper understanding of the underlying philosophy. Over the next ten years he shaped his philosophy around the concept he called System of Profound Knowledge' (Deming,1993, p.96). The four-mutually dependent elements he identified are:

- Appreciation for a system
- Knowledge about variation
- Knowledge of psychology
- Theory of knowledge

Some have found the term 'Profound Knowledge' a little awkward to accept. We should not allow this to be an obstacle to understanding. Each of the elements will be explained briefly below, with a later reference to OFSTED and how this philosophy relates to the OFSTED process. It is important to point out that all the aspects of the 'System of Profound Knowledge' are intensely interrelated and this, in fact, is its robust uniqueness.

Deming's philosophy

(a) Appreciation for a system

All organisations form a system of interrelated components. Systems methodology teaches how to optimise each part of the system for the improvement of the whole.

The school system must have a purpose (or aim) – there is no system if there is no purpose or aim. To achieve real quality, each element must see its relationship to the others and to the whole, and the effect of working to achieve its own goals at the expense of optimising the system as a whole. System thinking involves understanding the interdependence of functions and people. Such thinking gives us the means to deploy policies which relate to our aims, where the aim gives the life force for all its policies and practices.

All the stakeholders of a school need to recognise its aims as having meaning and relevance to them, since they will be instrumental in bringing about 'success'. Only when this 'system view' is achieved can we ensure that the aims are being lived daily in everything that is done. For too many schools, the aims are merely a list of wishes.

(b) Knowledge about variation

It is essential to understand the variability of processes and how to minimise the variation to achieve consistency.

There is variation in all things, yet we run our schools as if no variation exists. Any process is subject to variation, so why do we cheer when exam results are high one year and despair when they are lower the next if the same process produced both? Such variability will always be present. We do not ignore this, however. Rather than reacting to single data points, we analyse the processes which produce the data. This methodology is as appropriate to behaviour issues and learning progress as it is to managerial and administrative issues.

(c) Knowledge of psychology

This involves understanding motivation and optimisation of all people in an organisation in order to galvanise improvement and innovation.

There is faulty thinking in many schools regarding human motivation. We still operate as though we can somehow inject motivation into people. In reality, what we should aim for is the release of intrinsic motivation through the systematic improvement of the circumstances in which people work. Real improvement can only be achieved with the participation of those involved. Much current policy centres around increasing competition. This 'win/lose' approach results in sub-optimisation of the system, due to lack of co-operation and sharing. 'Win/win' is a more powerful philosophy for improvement.

These theories are just as applicable to the classroom setting as to the whole school. Pupils are working within processes which, too often, crush out intrinsic motivation whilst enhancing competition. We need to spend less time 'pushing' people, including pupils, and more time removing the barriers to self-motivation, and encouraging co-operative learning. It is important to remember that improvement in the process or system will liberate people to do work of which they can be proud.

(d) Theory of knowledge

This requires an understanding of the importance of prediction to bring about improvement. How do we really know we are improving? A rigorous cycle of planning applied improvement efforts is one of the main features.

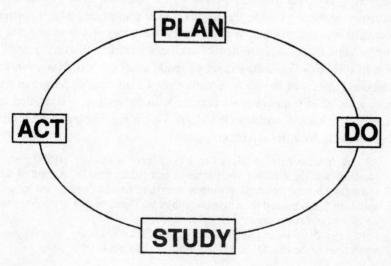

Figure 6.1

The Plan, Do, Study, Act cycle (Neave 1990, pp139-49; Deming 1993, pp134-36) is rigorously applied to enable prediction of processes. Study, in Deming's terms, means analyse the process which is being implemented, collect appropriate data and evaluate what these data are telling you; i.e. 'What did we learn?' It takes us far beyond other school planning, which tends to go no further than identifying success criteria, setting a target and identifying the person responsible. Specifying a target in this way cannot guarantee that it is achieved. Understanding clearly what we are talking about (defining issues operationally), the processes involved and what they are capable of producing is vital. Ready, fire, aim! This is too often what characterises school planning.

Deming's philosophy and OFSTED

So how does OFSTED's approach and Deming's philosophy fit together? It has to be stated at the outset that there is much that schools have gained from the OFSTED *Framework* and *Handbook*. It has been described as one of the best INSET manuals ever produced (by accident!) in that it provides a clear set of indicators of what good practice might look like, whether you are in a highly selective grammar school in the leafy suburbs, or an inner-city school struggling with low aspirations and poor economic circumstances. What it does not do is provide any indication of how to become a school exhibiting good practice.

OFSTED's stated purpose is 'Improvement through Inspection'. Deming's response to this is expressed clearly in the opening paragraph to this chapter – 'By what method?'. Over recent years we have watched LEA advisory services provide the means and the strategies which teachers have put into practice across the country. Certainly, it would be naive to suggest that these improvements have been manifest in every school or that further improvements cannot be made in all schools. However, the-sustained efforts of the professionals over a considerable period of time have resulted in improvements nationally in the quality of education and standards achieved (without OFSTED). This is highlighted in the following comment from John Abbott:

> 'O' levels were first introduced in 1951. There were only 16,500 possible candidates in the then grammar schools and public schools. A third of them left school before they took the exam; one third passed three or less subjects, and only 5,500 passed four or more subjects. These people are now in their early 60s, and at the top of their professions.
>
> In 1992, 507,100 pupils took GCSE, and 358,400 got five or more passes equivalent to the old 'O' level (DfE statistics). (Abbott 1994, p51)

OFSTED's approach – more akin to 'hit and run' than advice and support – will not, in itself, bring about improvement. Earley, Fidler and Ouston (1995, p21) reported that: 'Teachers welcomed the advice offered but felt a degree of frustration that the inspection was not necessarily to be followed by support or INSET'. Some (even many) inspections have provided insights into strategies for improvement. This has often been the case where current (or former) LEA advisers have formed inspection teams and have given valuable verbal feedback. This 'off-the-record' feedback has sometimes proved more valuable to teachers than the formal, written report, where these inspectors have had to be guarded against giving advice. 'Improvement through inspection – but let's give the important advice on how to improve, as long as we're not caught doing it!'

OFSTED's own system handicaps the inspectors from giving the advice needed to improve, unless they choose to do otherwise covertly. Imagine taking your car to a garage and the mechanic says 'Your engine isn't running effectively – the fuel system is working at 80 per cent capacity'. Does this tell you how to improve the situation? Would you part with money for this report and feel satisfied?

The evidence from schools shows that there is considerable variation in inspection teams (as Deming would have predicted). Inspection is not a precise science, despite an apparently thorough set of guidelines. The judgements are made on outputs only, with no consideration of the processes which produce these outputs. This reflects a simplistic paradigm that the sum of the components identified is equal to the whole (e.g. resources + homes + teaching = output). In fact, the situation is infinitely more complex. The more realistic paradigm involves recognising that the whole is greater than simply the sum of its parts, that the output (say, learning) is a consequence of the (unknown) multiplicity of interactions between the contributory factors.

The difficulty OFSTED has with this view is that the quality of learning cannot be deduced by somehow measuring the contributory factors. Indeed, if we were to ask neuroscientists how to measure learning they would say that they do not know. OFSTED inspectors would be forced into pointing at several hundred inspection reports which clearly state that this is possible and that it can be given a grade! Quantifying resources (how many books in the library) is easy. Evaluating the effectiveness of their use (how their use contributes to learning) is less easy, but more important. In this we have a good example of regarding as important that which is measurable, rather than attempting to measure that which is important.

Yet judgements are sacrosanct, and are published without any recognition of their validity or the variation in their production. Despite this variation, most teams have been sensitive to the situation teachers are finding themselves in, whilst others (thankfully the minority) have inspected as though they were wearing jackboots under their suits. These have been cold, unprofessional occasions, producing unnecessary trauma for staff.

(a) Lack of understanding of system

Ted Wragg, writing about the National Curriculum in the *Times Educational Supplement*, set out the basis for this lack of understanding of system when he wrote:

> The trouble with locking ten groups of people away in different rooms is that they often have no idea what the other groups are doing and what emerges, therefore, has no coherence. (*TES*, 25 February 1994)

The OFSTED model of inspection is based on this concept. Subject inspectors are required to consider the quality of teaching, the quality of learning and the standards achieved in each subject area separately. Admittedly, certain important issues are considered across subject boundaries, but the bulk of a report comprises these separate subject commentaries.

In addition, the response to inspection of separate subject areas may increase the pressure for staff to respond in a way which may not best serve the needs of the pupils. For example, arbitrary targets may be set, and departments may strive to improve their performance by working even harder. This may be a worthy step until considered more carefully. If the system cannot deliver the arbitrary targets, the only result can be stress and a sense of failure (and, maybe, a scapegoat). Working to achieve improvement in your own area may have a negative effect on other departments and on pupils. If this sounds implausible, consider the competing demands on the time of secondary pupils as staff prepare them for exams. Pupils suffer from over-demand for their time for coursework and revision sessions – all aimed at their benefit, of course.

If one accepts that the purpose of a school is to enhance learning, then any distraction to meet an isolated and imposed specification invites sub-optimisation. Consider the inordinate amount of documentation (both that which is required and that which is proffered), the veritable blossoming of displays, the painted toilets, etc. that greet an OFSTED inspection team. Can we really believe that other important priorities are not forfeited to achieve the desired impression?

Many schools that have experienced an OFSTED inspection, including those with good and outstanding reports, will verify the stress and exhaustion which accompanies the process. Indeed, the 'post-OFSTED' syndrome seems to be a very real phenomenon. The experience, apart from the human costs, results in less energy for rigorous improvement, less innovation (because of the fear of not conforming) and more excuses for shelving important projects.

Everyone in education knows that the total educational experience for each child is unique, and is also greater than the sum of the parts (as already mentioned). In other words, the educational experience is a complex system, made up of many processes, which support and contribute to the aim or purpose. The OFSTED model has difficulty in viewing schools from this holistic approach, and this became very obvious when the secondary, subject-dominated model was applied to primary schools – and had problems!

A similar problem has occurred where secondary schools have taken an integrated approach to curriculum delivery, including elements of several curriculum areas in a package which is aimed at enhancing continuity, progression and security for its pupils. Inspection of such an area by separate subject inspectors has not provided a complete picture, nor an accurate evaluation of its performance.

Again it has to be said that the OFSTED *Framework* and *Handbook* have provided some very good INSET materials for schools and their advisers. However, the approach and application of this model of inspection is inadequate in viewing schools from a systems point of view. The resulting judgements can only be made by inspecting the parts and assuming the whole is simply the sum of them. We know that this approach would not build us a satisfactory motor car – yet the system of education in a school is far more complex (and important) than manufacturing motor cars.

Peter Sengé in his book *The Fifth Discipline*, encapsulated this aspect of Deming's philosophy:

> Systems thinking is a discipline for seeing wholes. It is a framework for seeing interrelationships rather than things, for seeing patterns of change rather than static 'snapshots'. (Sengé 1990, p68)

(b) Lack of knowledge about variation

Sengé's comment on 'snapshots' being an inadequate means of understanding systems sadly describes OFSTED's attention to a school. The consequence of 'snapshot' inspections is that schools are forced into reacting to single data points, observed during two days (the typical length of time a subject inspector spends in a secondary school), rather than collecting evidence and data over a longer period of time. This is not a desirable situation. Aspects of a school's performance such as the number of library books, pupil attendance and examination results may require a response in an Action Plan, though the data may not be clearly understood with respect to the normal variation produced by that process.

OFSTED allows for no understanding of in-process variation in inspection of a school nor, indeed, in its own processes. Inspection cannot be as uniform as the *Framework* suggests, though allowance has not been made for the variation which is known to exist between and within teams. Many of the anecdotal examples shared between teachers and other colleagues will bear testimony to this. Any observation is subjective ('what is good'?). This is one of the false premises of OFSTED, that it is an objective and accurate system of measurement. Moderation procedures would help to minimise this variation, but only if this is done with a full understanding of variation, the data which should be collected for analysis, and the techniques for analysis of that data. More fundamentally, a reappraisal of the system and its purpose would be of greater benefit than trying to improve one which cannot achieve its declared purpose (Einstein's notion of not solving problems with the same thinking we used when we created them).

(c) Psychology

The impact of OFSTED inspections has been traumatic for many teachers. Inspection is a stressful event – the public judgement, regardless of context, of a private profession – based on the premise that exposure will bring about the motivation to improve. What evidence supports this notion that fear is the best motivator? At best fear will bring about temporary compliance, but will have only a negative effect on innovation and intrinsic motivation. For a full account of this concept see *Punished by Rewards* by Alfie Kohn (1993).

How many teachers came into the profession to 'screw up'? How many come to school each day just to see if they can 'mess up' the learning process or the school's systems? It is all too easy for OFSTED's judgements to be used to find scapegoats, promoting a 'blame culture' in our schools, rather than a culture of professional development, honesty and innovation. Whilst attempting to foster a climate of challenge and innovation for our youngsters, teachers are being treated with an outmoded view of motivation in order to encourage them to 'deliver the goods'.

Outcomes of such an approach to motivation might include taking short-cuts to produce more icing on the cake rather than a better cake. Such superficial improvements might include bringing about an improvement in the published exam grades A to C through revision clubs designed to increase the number of C grades. This happens at the expense of improved learning opportunities for all pupils; pupils who cannot obtain C grades feel devalued and demotivated (with all the ensuing problems which may then arise). Similar responses can be discovered for almost any example of arbitrary judgements or targets and their publication in reports.

The premise that exposure, by increasing competition, brings about improvement is also a fallacy. Competition inhibits sharing of good practice and promotes a win/lose mentality. In our education system who are to be the losers? Thank goodness most professionals decry this and participate in much valued sharing and mutual support (win/win). The whole concept of league tables and end of process inspection leads to the response of 'working to the targets' as opposed to improving learning and thus serving the real purpose of the school. Ranking and rating will not bring about improvement. Such an approach focuses on the efforts of the people and does not recognise or understand their interactions with or the effects of the system in which they operate.

(d) Lack of a theory of knowledge (and improvement)

Improvement through inspection is, in fact, improvement without theory. A methodology for process improvement is required, rather than a criticism of the outcomes of processes.

Generally the OFSTED model will seek evidence that something is happening, and will make a judgement of its effectiveness. What OFSTED does not go on to say is how the required improvement should be brought about. This advice may, of course, be bought from any of the LEA or freelance advisers on the 'free' market – the very same people who are now inspecting schools (at considerable cost), but are not allowed to give the advice which is needed by the schools.

How can Deming's philosophy bring about improvement in our schools?

This is the question which is being investigated in a handful of schools in the Midlands. In 1992, an association between two organisations – The British Deming Association and The Regional Staff College – enabled this work to begin. The BDA was formed in 1987 by organisations and individuals who had gained fresh insight into their approach to management through the work of Deming. The association exists to spread awareness of the Deming management philosophy and to help members put it into practice. It is located in Salisbury, Wiltshire. The Regional Staff College was set up in 1986 to provide management training opportunities for teachers throughout the West Midlands, and is situated in Dudley.

Together, these two organisations considered ways of helping schools learn more about Deming's work, and to see how it can help them improve. A series of seminars was designed and delivered to groups of senior managers from schools in the region, with resounding success. However, it was clear that seminars alone would not provide sufficient learning opportunities for these managers to develop capability themselves, nor to develop the capabilities of the rest of the staff in the school. Neither was a series of seminars going to have the desired impact on classroom practice, to improve the quality of learning and to help pupils become engaged in learning.

In order to develop a better understanding of this process of transformation, it was decided that the best way to move further forward would be to identify a small number of pilot schools and provide them with support. The schools selected for the pilot scheme represented a range of types of institution including state schools from the primary, secondary, and special school sectors, comprehensive and selective schools, and one independent school. An appetite for change was, of course, a necessary prerequisite.

At the time of writing, these schools are being provided with the training and support necessary for them to learn and implement Deming's philosophy. Each school chosen (from those who submitted an application), is provided with seminars and support by two mentors selected by the BDA. One of these mentors has specific and proven expertise in Deming's work, whilst the other either works in or has a background in education, as well as having an understanding of and commitment to Deming's philosophy. With this balance of Deming 'expert' and educationalist, it was intended that the schools would have mentors who could not only provide learning opportunities, but also understand the context of schools.

The purpose of the pilot scheme was to demonstrate that applying Deming's thinking to educational processes can enhance learning – to prove that there is a better way to develop life-long learners. The educational processes in question include any and all of the processes in the school system, since all have an impact on learning. These include the management process as well as the learning processes. The terms of reference of the pilot scheme were made clear at the outset. Schools had to accept that this was to be a journey not a programme. They would be involved in directing the course and the pace of the transformation, and each school might well be different in these respects. It was clearly to be their change initiative.

The commitment from the pilot schools was for a 'critical mass' group to attend the education programme, to ongoing learning (including reading and self-development), and to share the processes and the results with other schools. The mentors made their own commitment. This included the provision of the education programme, periodic advice, and the facilitation of networking and mutual learning opportunities with others in the pilot. It was also made clear that a number of things were not on offer – money, staffing, a recipe book, 'bolt on' techniques, better league table position, and, in Deming's own words, 'Instant Pudding' (there would be no quick way out of any perceived or real crisis).

The Project has structure as well as purpose. The outline strategy involves a number of areas which are mapped over a period of time. The precise sequence and timing of these areas is at the discretion of the school – the ownership of the transformation is theirs. Elements of the strategy follow Deming's PDSA cycle (Figure 6.1) and are outlined in Figure 6.2.

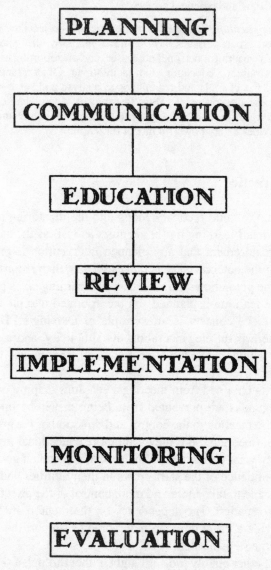

Figure 6.2

The approach involves three main areas of development and activity which run concurrently:

Strategic Plan This involves the initial stage of identification of stakeholders in the school and their expectations, leading to the production of a purpose statement which is known to everyone. Also the schools revisit their vision and values, agree key success factors, and produce an outlined timetable for planned progress.

Learning The programme of education seminars provides the backbone of the formal learning, with the mentors filling in the gaps through discussion, directed reading and practical projects.

Practical applications Included here are practical projects to develop understanding of process issues. These have included the establishment of processes for meetings, personal processes, and the reporting of interventions (including training, education and facilitation). Other practical activities include the use of tools and techniques to analyse and solve problems, and effect process improvement. This 'learning by doing' has enabled sound understanding of the methodology in the context of the Deming's philosophy. It provides a very powerful model for learning.

PDSA in practice

It is important to build feedback loops into the mentoring process. This enables continual learning by the mentors as well as the staff involved. There is a requirement that any planned intervention is preceded by a prediction of the outcome. The actual events are then recorded and compared with the prediction – this is where the learning takes place. Finally action on the learning is planned and incorporated into the next planned intervention. The concept is an example of Deming's PDSA cycle in practice. There is an elegance about its simplicity, and a power in its application which helps the user focus on continuous learning and improvement.

Feedback is obtained from meetings, enabling shaping of their future direction. Agendas are prevented from being driven by one individual. This opens the meeting to the control and direction of the group – it truly becomes their meeting. So if they want more educational inputs they can say so; if they want more practical help, on the agenda it goes; and so on.

As the confidence of the staff grows in their abilities and understanding they are able to take more and more control of the direction and pace of the transformation. The dependency on the mentors moves from the need to provide a programme to being able to support the learning and help clarify the steps needed.

The use of other quality tools is taught, either through a short course or through the medium of practical projects. The use of these tools in isola-

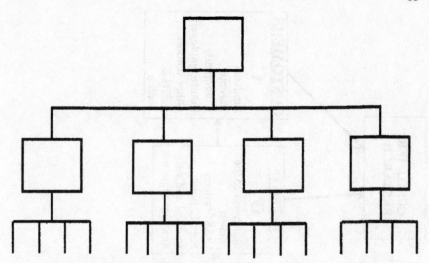

Figure 6.3 Generic organisation chart

tion of theory or philosophy (a feature of TQM, a term which Deming never used) has been avoided. Use of tools without focusing on the purpose of the organisation can lead to improvement, but can also be misinterpreted and the potential benefit may be lost. When these tools have been introduced in the schools, the prime purpose has been learning more of the application of the philosophy. Later, their use becomes integral to continuous improvement.

Deming's view of an organisation as a system is to the forefront in this work. When asked about their organisational structure, most managers will show a typical hierarchical chart similar to that in Figure 6.3. In our schools the boxes might contain subject areas, Key Stages or administrative functions. It is then possible for the manager to explain what the people assigned to these boxes are supposed to do. It is likely that each section's function can be described or fulfilled without reference to any other (hence the perceived need for cross-curricular approaches in schools).

Contrast this with Figure 6.4. This is a version of Deming's view of the organisation as a system as applied to a school.

Seen in this concept the purpose of the school is, in effect, the primary process, learning (and who can disagree with that?). It can also be seen quite clearly that all other elements in the existence of the school either contribute to or impinge upon the primary purpose of learning. It is this realisation which has been the cornerstone of transformation for some schools.

This approach has been applied with some success in the classroom, as the simplified example in Figure 6.5 shows. The question 'Has ability

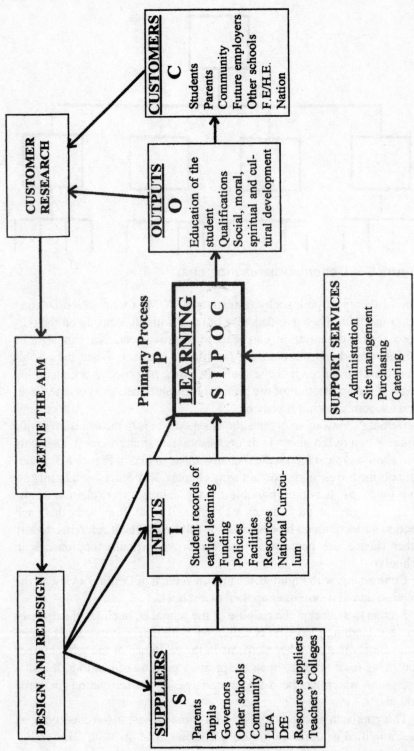

Figure 6.4 An organisation as a system applied to a school

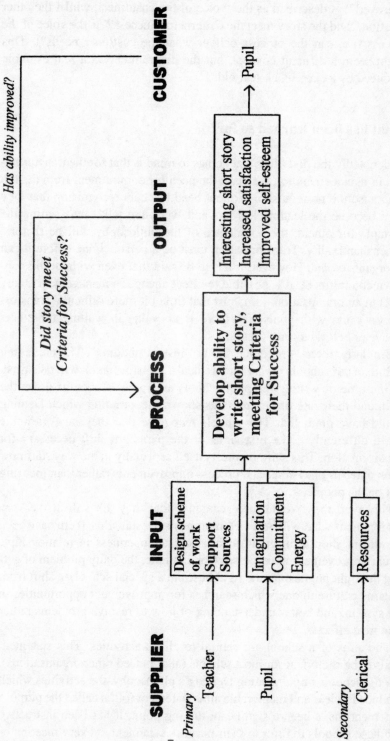

Figure 6.5 Simplified Process Diagram – Short Story Writing

improved?' is described as the 'voice of the customer', whilst the other question, 'Did the story meet the Criteria for Success?' is the voice of the process (i.e. can the process deliver what the customer needs?). This might seem a difficult concept, but the diagram shows a real example produced by a class of 11 year olds.

What has been learned so far?

Undoubtedly the first thing that comes to mind is that for the transformation in management to take place the need for commitment from the top is an absolute prerequisite. Without head teachers recognising that they must become the leading learners and 'walk the talk', thus setting the example for others, the acceptance of the philosophy will be rhetoric rather than reality. Transformation must be a personal one before it can be organisational. However, it has to be said that even without this top-down commitment, it is possible to effect change in management at any level in an organisation – it is just that little bit more difficult. Transformation starts with yourself – there is no value in waiting for others (above or below) to start first.

Similarly, there is no quick fix, no 'instant pudding'. The prevailing culture in our schools is very hierarchical – transformation will take time. At the time of writing the pilot schools are some 18 months down the road, and their rate of progress has shown the variation which Deming would have predicted. The schools recognise that they now view the world differently – the first signs of the paradigm shift necessary for transformation. This shift manifests itself especially in the way staff now think in terms of systems and process improvements rather than focusing just on the people.

However, they would also recognise that they are still at the very beginning of what will be a metamorphosis. Despite this, there have been significant short-term gains such as greater openness in relationships, actual improvement in processes (for example, the daily problem of getting the right pupils onto the right buses in a special school), a shift from a blame culture to one which searches for improvement opportunities in the system, and better understanding of how to resolve problems rather than treat effects.

The aims of a school are central to all its activities. This statement tends to be rhetorical for most schools (and, indeed other organisations). For the schools implementing Deming's philosophy, the activities which produced a clear and memorable aims statement (often called the purpose statement) have been a significant turning point. It has been instructive for these schools to refer to their purpose statement at every meeting or point in any decision-making process, to ensure that they are remaining true to their purpose in everything they do. This has not always been a comfortable position for them! However, it has helped them to focus on their activities in a new light – if it does not serve the purpose of the school, why are we doing it?

The mentoring process itself has exhibited variation and has needed to be flexible, responding to the changing and different needs of each school. All mentors are not the same and the approach they have used does not involve a recipe or check-list. Human relationships are notoriously complex and the relationships which have developed between the mentors and the colleagues in the schools have exhibited the variation expected in human characteristics. What has been common and of value has been the generic mentoring framework which has been used to guide the process rather than dictate it.

One of the most powerful modes of learning has been the process of 'learning by doing' which has enabled project teams in the schools to engage in practical process improvement whilst developing their understanding of 'Profound Knowledge'. The use of Deming's PDSA cycle of improvement has been the basis for this work. This discipline, coupled with sound application of tried and tested tools and techniques, has provided schools with a practical application of a profound philosophy, leading to fundamental rather than superficial improvement in management and operation. It has been important to ensure that such project teams are not seen as an exclusive club, with other staff regarding themselves as outsiders in the process. Good communication has been necessary.

Mentors have found that teachers like being taught! They have often been readily receptive to new concepts and strategies when they have been presented in the formal climate with which they are more familiar. It is interesting to note this implicit view of how learning best takes place, and reflect upon the recent research in brain-based learning as exemplified by Feuerstein in Israel and summarised by Jensen in America. The prospect of culture change has proved rewarding but challenging in the prevailing culture of the British education system, and has required regular contact in order to maintain commitment and prevent the activities being 'put on the back burner' because of the pace of today's educational climate.

It has been encouraging to hear the positive comments made by HMI during a visit to one of the pilot schools, and to consider one of the commonest concerns expressed by the teachers involved – 'When do we involve the pupils?'. By and large there have been two opposing views on this – either to wait until all (or at least most) of the staff have sufficient understanding themselves to enable transformation to take place in the learning processes, or to go out and do it and learn together. It is likely that the answer to this question will have more options than the two extremes described here. So far, few schools have linked the philosophy with the learning process in a practical way. Certainly, where individuals have 'gone out and done something' the responses from pupils have been encouraging. However, this approach does require that the teacher concerned has a good level of knowledge and is prepared to be brave in his or her classroom, for the positive responses are not universal in pupils (and parents), nor do they necessarily lie easily in the prevailing school culture.

Learning has not been confined to the schools. The mentors have also 'walked the talk' in meeting regularly to improve their activities. The generic mentoring process has undergone several manifestations and is continually reviewed as part of its own PDSA cycle. Out of the pilot scheme will come much knowledge about the opportunities and the obstacles to supporting schools in their desire for a transformation in the management of the organisation and in the learning process itself.

Imperatives for school management

It must come as no surprise that the writers would opine that managers should understand Deming's System of Profound Knowledge, and learn how to apply it to all that they do and are responsible for. Similarly, they should apply the concepts described in his '14 Points for Management' in the context of his philosophy. But what does this mean in practice?

Deming said that a manager should understand the meaning of a system and help their people to see themselves as components in it. They would help them to work in co-operation with preceding and succeeding stages, towards optimisation of the efforts of all stages, so as to achieve the aim. Without an aim there is no system. Management's job is to work on the system to improve it continually with the help of those who work in the system.

People are different from each other, and managers must recognise these differences, not only capitalising on them but also putting everybody in a position for development. This is not ranking of people but what, in the classroom, we call differentiation. We know it works there, we should apply it to management. This approach will help everybody to feel challenged and fulfilled. Such a manager will understand data and what they tell us, including the differences between variation which is part of the process and that which is outside the process.

A manager following Deming's philosophy will be a counsel and coach rather than a judge. A clear understanding of the differences between intrinsic and extrinsic motivation, and the effects they produce, will be used to the benefit of the organisation and its stakeholders. Trust will be created in an environment which encourages innovation. The ability to listen and learn will be a priority – in fact such a manager will be an unceasing learner, encouraging this trait in others. As Eric Hoffer has said:

'In times of change the learners will inherit the Earth, while the learned will find themselves beautifully equipped to deal with a world that no longer exists.' (In Barth, 1993.)

Continuous improvement will be emphasised, following a theory of knowledge and improvement – the PDSA cycle. Clear, unambiguous communications are vital to prevent misunderstandings. This may sound obvious until we actually try to operationally define what we are talking about. This involves defining what we are saying in the context of how it will be used.

Essentially the move should be from directive management to process management. Gone will be exhortations to motivate people, instead we shall be focused on removing the barriers to motivation. Instead of looking for someone to blame we shall be seeking process improvements. Decisions will be driven by theory and data rather than opinions and prejudice.

In this way will reactive crisis management move to proactive preventative management. It will not produce the same sort of excitement, for the manager who has succeeded through firefighting will lose that thrill. Instead there will be the more subtle and mature satisfaction of fireproofing. The essential precursor to this organisational transformation is personal transformation. It will not happen if everyone involved (especially the leaders of the transformation) do not recognise the need for the changes to be apparent in themselves first.

'Deming schools'

So how are 'Deming schools' different? What would characterise a school which has undergone such a transformation? Some indicators may be found in other schools, but the presence of the philosophy behind them is the significant factor. 'Many of Deming's ideas are not new, but perhaps we need to be challenged by old ideas in a new way from time to time' (Ouston 1995, p34).

A check-list of characteristics does not do justice to the paradigm shift seen in those schools involved. However, such a school exhibits constancy of purpose, with concentration on process improvement through people rather than concentrating on changing people. The school is described as a system and everyone understands their contribution. People are innovative in a climate free from fear, they understand motivation (intrinsic and extrinsic) and how to help staff and pupils gain satisfaction from what they do. The overriding principle is win/win and the enhancement of self-esteem. Relationships are focused to align 'best efforts' towards the purpose or aim.

Such schools exhibit a healthy scepticism to data, and a desire and capability to understand and interpret data sensibly. They learn to be cautious about reacting to single data points, but learn to identify process improvement opportunities. The use of scientific methodology (the PDSA cycle) in the planning of all activities is normal, as is the proper use of quality tools. 'Joy in work' is a reality for staff and students alike.

Conclusion

The coupling of Deming's philosophy with the recent research from around the world on how best the brain learns will provide possibly one of the greatest steps in human and organisational development the world has seen. We are on the edge of a new age of learning – it always takes courage to step into the unfamiliar.

Some things must change including sacred cows such as improvement through competition, improvement through exposure and ranking (e.g. league tables) and 'end-of-process' inspection. Others including reliance on 'carrot and stick' methods of motivation (which, in schools, we call 'rewards and punishment') must be challenged. Co-operative learning as opposed to competitive learning has shown itself to be of greater value academically and socially. Reliance on extrinsic motivators will bring about short term compliance, but will not engage students in learning for the rest of their lives. Removal of the barriers to enjoyment of learning will be a priority if we are to achieve some of the desired improvements in educational and social achievement. Working smarter rather than harder will be the new order. This will require better understanding of what makes learning effective rather than merely doing more of what has been seen to be effective so far.

> Existing systems produce existing ideas. If something different is required, the system must be changed. (Sir Christopher Ball, *More Means Different*, 1990 in Abbott, 1994, p.85.)

In order for schools to improve drastically, new behaviours will be necessary. These new behaviours will be based on a sound understanding of a philosophy for managing improvement, as well as the strategies to be applied to bring it about. It is our belief that the work currently being undertaken in some schools will provide evidence that this is the case.

In returning to the opening remarks of this chapter, it is, perhaps, instructive to consider the cost of an inspection of a typical secondary school. Some 45 inspector days are required to be spent on the inspection every four years. This would be the equivalent of 11 days per year for four years, i.e. one day per year per curriculum area. Would not the money spent on these end-of-process judgements be more wisely spent on advice and support for improvement, responding to Deming's profoundly simple question: 'By what method?'.

Note The British Deming Association can be contacted at The Old George Brewery, Rollestone Street, Salisbury, Wiltshire SP1 1DX. The Regional Staff College is working with the British Deming Association to co-ordinate Deming's work in schools nationally. Anyone interested in learning more or in sharing their experiences is invited to join a Deming Schools Network by writing to The Regional Staff College at Dudley, West Midlands DY3 4JH.

CHAPTER SEVEN

Developing the Effectiveness of Senior Management Teams through the Use of School Management Standards

by Gill Cleland

This chapter documents the trialling of a system of management review and improvement designed for senior management teams (SMTs). Although the trials took place in primary schools, the approach is likely to be equally applicable to schools in the secondary sector.

At a time when schools are seeking to adapt their management styles and structures to become more responsive in meeting the challenge of the post Education Reform Act market oriented world of education, the system described was designed to provide tools and processes to help SMTs to develop and demonstrate the characteristics of effective team and organisational management that are essential components of quality management systems.

The delivery of the system, in the form of school-based workshops over a period of three months, was followed up by head teacher interviews and participant questionnaires, an analysis of which demonstrates clear gains to schools in the areas of management team development, management process improvement and management skills development. It is suggested that adoption of the programme could help schools to take the first steps towards developing a quality management system.

Context and rationale

From September 1991 to March 1992 the writer was a member of the Working Party for the West Midlands Regional Collaborative Project on 'Profiling and Competences', funded by the School Management Task Force (SMTF) following the publication of its 1990 Report, *Developing*

School Management: The Way Forward. The outcome of the Project was the launch, in January 1993, of the University of Wolverhampton's School Management Development Programme (SMDP). This programme enables individual teachers in primary and secondary schools to develop their managerial skills in the context of their own school, in line with SMTF recommendations, and is based on the framework of school management standards (Annex 1 to this chapter) produced by the School Management Competences Project (Earley 1992b). After considerable success with the delivery of this programme of individual managerial development, it was felt appropriate to extend the approach to cater for the needs of management team development. There were several reasons for this:

- In the Final Report of the School Management Competences Project, Earley (1992a, p30) reported that amongst the specific benefits for schools of using the management standards were: enhancement of professional working relationships, contribution to team-building, and the provision of a mechanism for the review of school management.
- Other literature mentions the potential of using standards for teams as well as individuals. For example, Esp (1993, p138) suggests that where teams collaborate to produce portfolios of evidence of managerial competence this can lead to 'greater efficiency in achieving objectives and greater effectiveness as a working group'.
- As a by-product of the pilot work undertaken in schools during the West Midlands Consortium Project, several successful exploratory sessions were conducted with SMTs in primary and secondary schools, during which the standards proved useful as a means of promoting discussion and evaluation of various management processes.
- Senior managers in schools are currently concerned about the prospect of OFSTED inspection, leading them to seek tools and training which will help them to review their overall management processes systematically and develop improvement strategies which are clearly linked to OFSTED criteria. They seek, for example, a process which will supply evidence of 'the school's use of self-evaluation and analysis' (OFSTED 1993, Section 4, pp33-4).

From the above it can be seen that scope existed for the broadening of the individually focused School Management Development Programme to embrace the needs of senior management teams. The concept of Management Review and Improvement was therefore developed into a package of workshop sessions for senior managers, designed to address the growing emphasis upon self-review and evaluation as a means of achieving school improvement: an emphasis encouraged not only by OFSTED (ibid.), but also in *Learning to Succeed: Report of the National*

Commission on Education (National Commission on Education 1993), which urges the recognition of the central role of schools in evaluating their own performance and initiating improvements in response to identified needs. The process of review and evaluation undertaken during the workshop sessions was based on the use of Standards for School Management (Earley 1992b) in order to exploit their potential for promoting team-building, management process improvement and as a vehicle for the development of team skills.

Central to the development of the Management Review and Improvement system was the question of how to help SMTs to adopt working practices appropriate to the development of the kind of characteristics which emerge from the 'effectiveness' and 'quality' literature. Clearly, as Murgatroyd and Morgan (1993, p60) point out, quality and effectiveness require more than an intellectual commitment on the part of senior managers. There is a need for change in the way that actual processes are managed, since 'it is process quality and effectiveness that leads to sustainable quality outcomes'. It was felt that by basing the workshops on the use of a framework of management standards, SMTs would be encouraged to focus their attention and efforts on the enhancement of process quality by examining current practice against the performance criteria laid down in the Standards, identifying any areas of weakness and agreeing appropriate improvement strategies. In so doing, there would be opportunity for improving the quality of interaction, collaboration and co-operation within the team, as well as the management skills of individuals.

The trialling of the Management Review and Improvement system

The schools

The programme of Management Review and Improvement workshops was offered to primary schools local to the University of Wolverhampton, resulting in ten client schools for the academic year 1993–4. Of these ten, the two schools opting for delivery of the programme during the Spring Term, agreed to act as 'study schools'. Since the schools were paying clients and as such chose themselves, there could be no attempt to match them for size, catchment area, previous management INSET courses or indeed any other variables. Therefore there was no attempt to compare outcomes between the two study schools or to relate findings to particular characteristics of either of the schools.

By coincidence there were some similarities between the two study schools. The head teachers had both been in post for about seven years and both had attended a conference run by the University on the nature and purpose of Standards for School Management. Both schools had approximately 400 pupils on roll and both SMTs had nine members. In each case the head teacher had decided that although the SMT usually consisted of five people, the maximum benefit would be derived from the workshops by increasing the team size to include other significant postholders. There were several reasons for this. Firstly, as it was intended that the process of management review and improvement would eventually become the *modus operandi* of all staff, it was important from the outset to engage the commitment and support of everyone who would have a key dissemination role. Secondly, there was the recognition, supported by the SMTF Report, 1990, that management development should reach out to all concerned and not be confined to the most senior members of staff. Thirdly, at the level of value for money, the cost of the programme would be the same for a group of nine as for a smaller group.

The programme of workshops

The programme consisted of six twilight sessions of approximately 90 minutes delivered in each of the schools over a period of three months, on dates negotiated to fit in with the SMTs' existing schedule of after school meetings. The programme was not a course of lectures, though there was some provider input particularly in the first session. The intention was that once the tools and strategies had been explained and grasped, workshop sessions would involve the whole team in applying the processes to areas of management identified as appropriate by the team.

The six sessions of the programme

In the first session input was provided on the characteristics of effective schools, based on the work of Fullan (1992a), Mortimore et al. (1988), OFSTED (1993, 1994a), Preedy (1993), and SMTF (1990). The main purpose of the session was to provide a focus for initial discussion of managers' perceptions of their own school's current strengths and areas for development, which could be drawn upon in later sessions. A second purpose was to help the group and facilitator to get to know each other and start to build up an effective working relationship. Thirdly, although initial visits had been made to each school to meet the teams and discuss the programme, Session 1 was an opportunity to reaffirm the programme's rationale. After the initial input, participants worked in groups of three using the Halton Model (Fullan 1992a). Each group considered one of the segments of the model which presents characteristics of school effectiveness in three clusters, relating to: a common mission; emphasis on learning; and a climate conducive to learning. There was a sharing, within and between groups, of perceptions of the school's current level of effectiveness in relation to all three clusters of characteristics.

The outcome of this exploration of 'gut feelings' was the identification of 'teacher development' as an area worthy of further consideration by School A, while School B saw 'community involvement and the promotion of a more positive school image' as areas of concern. Both schools felt that 'monitoring' was an issue that could usefully be addressed. Thus each of the two SMTs had identified a clear focus around which the remaining workshops could be tailored.

In Session 2, the Standards for School Management (Annex 1), were introduced. Their nature, purpose and content were explained and explored. These were to become the tool through which the schools would adopt the process of Management Review and Improvement. As an initial exercise aimed at consolidating their understanding of the Standards, each participant completed a role analysis sheet, translating their job description into management tasks. This led to the compilation of a team management 'map', showing each person's responsibilities in relation to everyone else's. Agreement was then sought as to which management task areas should be used for the Management Review and Improvement process to be undertaken in Sessions 3 to 6.

In the light of their discussions in Session 1, School A decided to concentrate their review on Unit C2 of the Standards: 'Develop teams, individuals and self to enhance performance'. This would be followed by Unit B2: 'Monitor and evaluate learning programmes'. School B chose Unit A2: 'Develop supportive relationships with pupils, staff, parents, governors and the community', followed by Unit B2: 'Monitor and evaluate learning programmes'. Having thus translated the areas of concern identified in Session 1 into management tasks as defined by the Standards for School Management, both schools were now ready to consider the performance criteria attached to the Standards to start the process of systematic review of current practice and identification of improvement strategies in their chosen areas.

In Sessions 3 to 6 the work focused on an in-depth review of the areas. Current school procedures were discussed and analysed against the relevant performance criteria set out in the Standards for School Management. Improvement strategies and goals were then agreed and recorded on a specially designed planning pro-forma. Care was taken to ensure that any proposed targets were SMART (Specific, Measurable, Achievable, Realistic, Timed). No target was recorded without due consideration of the need to allocate responsibility within the team for co-ordinating and overseeing progress towards its achievement. Like-wise the resource implications of each target were explored before any commitment was agreed. The facilitator's role during these sessions was to clarify the terminology of the Standards where necessary, to stimulate discussion by posing questions, to act as note taker and to prepare draft versions of the review record for subsequent agreement or amendment.

Feedback and data collection

It was agreed that verbal feedback would be obtained by means of semi-structured interviews with the two head teachers, the purpose being to explore whether or not they felt that the workshops had proved beneficial in the three key areas of: management team development; management process improvement; management skills development. The interviews took place during the week following completion of the workshops, enabling a short period of reflection to occur and allowing time for the head teachers to hold a debriefing meeting with their teams.

The use of a questionnaire to supplement and help verify or refute the head teacher interview data was seen as appropriate. Following the head teacher interviews and the resulting analysis of their views, a two-part questionnaire was constructed, with the agreement that all members of the two participating SMTs would complete it.

The ten statements constituting Part A of the questionnaire (Annex 2 to this chapter) were constructed to reflect the areas in which the head teacher feedback appeared to be indicating positive effects derived from the work-shop programme. The purpose of Part B (Annex 3) was to explore the impact of the programme on the development of the skills and attitudes of effective teams since the literature on effective school management indicates the crucial importance of effective teamwork in influencing management quality. It seemed appropriate, therefore, to present a set of team effectiveness characteristics derived from the literature (Riches 1993, p13; West-Burnham 1991, p52) and to invite participants to assess the impact of the workshops in reinforcing their ability to display them.

Analysis of feedback

1. Management team development

Head teachers indicated that, in their view, the Management Review and Improvement process had helped teams to work more productively together. One reason for this was the involvement of an external facilitator who could question, coach, lead, keep people on task and inject fresh ideas. Analysis of the questionnaire data showed that eight out of ten team members strongly supported this feeling.

The 'Effective Management in Schools' project (Bolam et al. 1993), emphasised the need for SMTs to work together well and have clear roles and responsibilities. In the two study schools the workshop process had a very positive effect in encouraging co-operation and collaboration, with 15 of the 18 participants reporting that the impact in this area had been high. Head teachers cited the active involvement of all members of the team as an important factor here. However, it is interesting to note that although head teachers felt that the process had given all members some responsibility and that there had been an increase in the feeling of mutual support and understanding, the team members' response showed that whilst nearly three quarters felt that the programme's impact on shared decision-making and consensus seeking was high, the remainder had reservations here. It must be remembered that in both schools several teachers had been co-opted onto the SMT for the duration of the workshops and it is possible that they felt some insecurity and reticence in working with more experienced 'regular' members of the team, when it came to decision-making.

Despite the high level of team members' agreement that the workshops had facilitated co-operative and collaborative working, none felt that there had been a high impact in the area of making the best use of the qualities and experience of each team member. Although exactly half of them felt that the impact had been significant, three gave it a low rating of only 2 on the 5 to 1 scale. One possible reason for this was, again, the fact that the teams contained newly co-opted members whose potential had yet to make itself apparent. Another reason could have been that the workshop facilitator did not know the individuals well enough to ensure that the potential contribution of each one was fully explored and exploited. Despite the well documented advantages of using external 'experts' as facilitators (e.g. Aguayo 1990), their full impact may depend quite significantly on the extent and depth of pre-INSET communication between facilitator and clients. Although both schools were visited prior to the programme and team composition was discussed, more time should have been devoted to this aspect of preparation.

In terms of having clear roles and responsibilities, all team members agreed or strongly agreed that the workshops had increased their knowledge and understanding of the tasks involved in managing the school and that they had also gained a clearer understanding of the management tasks involved in their own role. Head teachers' views supported this in that they felt that there had been an increased overall understanding of the tasks to be undertaken and that individual team members' ability to define their own management task responsibilities had improved. In the opinion of one head teacher the charting of each team member's role on an overall management task framework had engendered a feeling of team spirit and interdependence.

For teams to work well together they need clear goals and development strategies. It is evident that the use of Standards for School Management was very significant in helping the teams to identify improvement needs and set realistic goals and that the nature of the workshop process had a high level of impact on their ability to formulate clear objectives and strategies for working towards these goals. All participants agreed or strongly agreed that this was the case. Head teachers also felt that the use of the Standards had generated clear goals and had maintained sharply focused discussion. Most team members felt that the Standards had made the review process logical and straightforward, and the view of one head teacher was that 'without this logical way of working we could have waffled on for ages'. It would also appear that success in enabling clear goals and strategies to be identified had a positive effect on the teams' willingness to take action and make things happen, as the majority of participants reported a high impact in this area.

2. Management process improvement

Head teachers felt that the adoption of the Standards as a basis for review and improvement had the potential to improve process management generally. This was because of the ease with which these tools would enable teams to maintain a clear overview of what needed to be done and provide the means of tracking and assessing progress. The systematic nature of the process was seen as a means of ensuring the quality of actions taken. In support of this optimistic view of the level of process improvement that continued use of the system would bring, team members' responses showed that nearly all agreed or strongly agreed that the Standards-based approach would enhance the long-term management effectiveness of the team. This supports the view that team use of Standards could provide a useful focus and stimulus for the review of current effectiveness and the identification of areas for quality improvement. The ultimate test of the system's value would be in its potential to make a positive impact on the management of teaching and learning, since this is at the heart of the purpose of school management. All but one of the workshop participants felt that the review and improvement process had already demonstrated its potential in this respect.

Both schools achieved concrete gains in process improvement. These were:

- a Staff Development Policy (School A);
- a Curriculum Monitoring Policy (both schools); and
- a development strategy for promoting the school's image and closer links with the community (School B).

In working towards achieving these improvements, appropriate sections of the OFSTED *Framework for the Inspection of Schools* were examined and responses showed that nearly all participants agreed or strongly agreed that linking Management Standards with OFSTED criteria had been useful. Head teachers appreciated the way that this had helped team members to start to develop their knowledge and understanding of the OFSTED *Framework* and its management implications, and saw the Standards approach as a key tool in systematically addressing all the OFSTED requirements over a period of time.

Achieving tangible improvements in management processes had a confidence boosting effect on the two management teams. The majority felt strongly that their confidence in their ability to manage the school effectively had been enhanced, and everyone had derived a significant or strong sense of enjoyment and satisfaction from working together as a team. Head teachers expressed the confidence building effect of the process improvements in terms of 'having a management tool that makes us feel empowered to act' and 'a feeling that we can achieve anything we set our collective minds to'.

Process improvement appears to have been facilitated by use of the Review and Improvement record sheets designed especially for the programme. Head teachers felt that the recording process and compilation of a Record of Management Review file had provided a sense of purpose, progress and achievement, and nearly all team members supported this view.

3. Management skills development

Both head teachers considered a good knowledge base to be the most important 'skill' that successful SMTs could possess and thought that participants had made significant strides in knowledge and understanding of management tasks and processes as a result of the workshops. The team members' feedback fully supported the view that knowledge and understanding of tasks and roles had been considerably enhanced.

Head teachers were optimistic that a good knowledge base would lead senior managers to develop and display other skills necessary for dynamic team activity. They saw confidence as a particular 'skill' already fostered through the programme and were able to give examples of individuals whose confidence had received a particular boost. As noted earlier, there was a clear link between process improvement and confidence building, and one head teacher saw confidence manifested as excitement and a feel-good factor, derived from the realisation that the team's current practice in many areas of management already almost matched the performance criteria.

In the opinion of head teachers, improved knowledge and confidence were starting to have a positive effect on the attitude, drive and commitment of team members to the extent that Head teacher A's team felt 'geared up' and 'invigorated', whilst Head teacher B felt that his team had become 'hooked on self-improvement and the quest for quality'. Team members' views support these perceptions in that their responses indicated that the impact of the workshops on the majority of them had been high in encouraging them to show drive, a sense of purpose and commitment to development.

The processes involved in the workshops were designed to promote the development of the skills of reviewing and reflecting upon current management practice, identifying areas for development and agreeing appropriate targets and strategies. The feedback was very encouraging in these areas, with almost all team members reporting a high level of impact on their team's willingness to adopt a self-critical and self-evaluative approach to school improvement, and a similar effect on their ability to show a positive attitude to identifying problems and seeking solutions.

Communication skills, crucial to co-operative and collaborative team work, appeared to have been stimulated through the workshop programme, with all participants perceiving a very significant impact on their team's ability to communicate effectively with each other in an open and honest way and on their willingness to participate in discussion.

Although the majority of participants felt that the workshops had had some significance in terms of encouraging flexibility in coping with change, the impact was not perceived as high. Possible reasons could be, firstly, that they felt that their degree of flexibility was already so well developed as a result of all the change that they have had to cope with since the Education Reform Act of 1988, that there was no scope for improvement in this respect! Secondly, as the workshops consisted of only six sessions over a three month period, the need for coping skills to implement proposed development plans had yet to be addressed. Thirdly, as the programme encouraged small incremental steps towards improvement in management practice, the need to display coping skills was also gradual and low key. In other words, by embracing the Japanese philosophy of 'Kaizen', the process of 'continuous improvement' on which the workshops were based could be achieved without peaks of stress and upheaval.

As regards the programme's ability to encourage the articulation of shared values and beliefs, reactions were varied, with just over one third of team members reporting a high level of impact. For the remaining two thirds some impact was experienced, albeit to a lesser degree. Perhaps some felt that the management areas upon which they concentrated during the workshop sessions did not impinge significantly on shared values and beliefs, even though one head teacher reported that a significant benefit had been 'enlightenment as to what we are all working towards to ensure our school aims are delivered'. It is true, however, that the workshop sessions did not perhaps allow sufficient opportunity for discussion of values and beliefs underlying the schools' aims, and tended to concentrate efforts on familiarising participants with tools and processes. Certainly, in the main, review of current practices tended to concentrate on 'what we do now' and 'how we do it now', rather than addressing the question 'why do we do it this way?'. Asking this question could have stimulated discussion on values and beliefs, for, as Murgatroyd and Morgan (1993, pp63–6) assert, it is '**Vision**', in the sense of the articulation of shared values and beliefs, that lies at the very heart of quality management.

Summary of significant outcomes

From the foregoing analysis it is fair to conclude that the factors which led the two SMTs to perceive that the Management Review and Improvement programme had been beneficial were:

1 Management team development

    (a) Support of an external 'expert'.
    (b) Provision of tools to facilitate the review and improvement process.
    (c) Setting of clear goals and implementation strategies.
    (d) Sharply focused and purposeful discussion.
    (e) Active involvement of all members of the team.

2 Management process improvement

    (a) Achievement of concrete outcomes or products in the chosen areas of focus.
    (b) Adoption of Standards for School Management as a means of identifying areas for quality improvement and to monitor and measure progress.

3 Management skills development

The factors listed in 1 and 2 above led to increases in:
    (a) Knowledge and understanding of management tasks and processes.
    (b) Ability to adopt a reflective and evaluative approach to management.
    (c) Managerial confidence, drive and commitment.
    (d) Willingness to identify problems and seek solutions.
    (e) Effective listening and communication, and willingness to engage in discussion.

Areas for improvement

There were three ways in which the impact and benefits of the workshop programme could have been increased. There was a need to:

(a) Ensure that all members of the teams felt comfortable and confident enough to participate in shared decision-making.
(b) Recognise and make better use of the qualities and experiences of each team member.
(c) Spend more time relating the Management Review and Improvement process to the schools' vision and ethos.

Towards quality management of schools

The reforms of the education service in the 1980s and the emergence of the market economy in which responsibility, authority and accountability have been shifted to institutional level, have produced major changes. School managers are increasingly under pressure to develop more sophisticated strategies to respond to what Sallis (1991) has described as the need to reconcile strategies which deal with competition and survival on the one hand, with the imperative of meeting client needs on the other hand, whilst at the same time ensuring that all actions are rooted in and compatible with the key purposes of education. A number of writers, for example Murgatroyd and Morgan (1993), Sallis (1991, 1993), and West-Burnham (1991) have suggested that what are becoming known as 'quality approaches' may be a vehicle for schools to manage themselves effectively in a time of rapid change. However, West-Burnham (1991, pp47–8) warns that the traditional educational perception of quality as an ideal 'which we can only ever aspire to' is no longer acceptable. What is required are tangible definitions of quality and criteria by which quality can be managed and measured. If schools wish to adopt a quality approach, the standards against which quality is to be measured must be comprehensive enough to incorporate the 'products' and 'services' of all members of the staff team, indicate who the stakeholders for each of these might be, and provide performance criteria which will enable quality service to be measured and demonstrated, whilst allowing at the same time some flexibility for individuals to interpret the means of achievement. It is fair to suggest that the success of the Management Review and Improvement process owed much to the fact that the tools used – namely the framework of Standards for School Management in conjunction with guidance from the OFSTED *Handbook* and from the school effectiveness literature – provided schools with clear and realistic criteria against which quality improvement goals could be set and measured.

Although the literature does not offer a single universal theory of quality management and suggests an adaptable concept which can evolve to fit the context of specific organisations, there appear to be some underlying key imperatives for quality approaches. The model for Total Quality Management in the school, proposed by Murgatroyd and Morgan (1993, pp 63–7) suggests that successful implementation of a quality management approach depends on the following five key features:

1. Shared **Vision**, with everyone pulling in the same direction.
2. Challenging **Goals** designed to move the organisation forward.
3. **Strategy** based on a shared understanding of the customer-driven and process-oriented basis for quality.
4. Use of **Teams** as the basis of the organisation's activity.
5. Systematic management through the use of **Tools** for measurement and feedback.

It is suggested that if the quality approach is to succeed, the senior management team must take responsibility for ensuring that all five of these essential elements are put in place and maintained. Furthermore, the effectiveness of the five elements requires the support of three implicit qualities of the organisation, referred to as the three C's of **Culture, Commitment** and **Communication.**

The following brief examination of the outcomes of the Management Review and Improvement system indicates that the process achieved significant success in establishing the first steps towards the development of a quality system in terms of Murgatroyd and Morgan's essential elements.

Vision Although the programme as delivered did make some impact in encouraging the articulation of shared values and beliefs, hindsight suggests that more emphasis could usefully have been placed on ensuring that agreed goals arose from and were compatible with the school's ethos. The danger was, that without such a focus, the Standards for School Management could have been allowed to dictate rather than support policy.

Teams The programme made a significant impact on the team's ability to co-operate and collaborate productively. The effect could have been further enhanced if more time had been spent in studying the composition of the teams to ensure that each individual's experience and expertise was fully used.

Strategy and Goals The use of Standards for School Management was seen as very effective in enabling improvement goals to be identified and implementation strategies to be agreed, monitored and measured. It is generally accepted that for a team to be successful it is crucial for members to have definite tasks and to understand what they are trying to achieve (Drucker 1990). The need for the team to have a shared understanding of the expected outcomes and a feeling of collective responsibility in working on a joint enterprise (West-Burnham 1991), appears to have been met for the two senior management teams.

Tools In addition to the Standards for School Management, the use of a role analysis and mapping process, and of the review and improvement record sheets were viewed as instrumental in encouraging effective team work and the identification and realisation of agreed goals. The initial audit process made good use of the OFSTED inspection guidance as a tool for school self-evaluation, and, together with the lists of effectiveness criteria derived from the research literature, this provided a valuable framework to facilitate the establishment of development priorities.

Commitment, Communication, Culture The feedback from both head teachers and senior management team members gave very clear indications that the nature and format of the workshop programme had a significant impact in respect of each of these skills and attitudes that supply the linkage between the other key elements of Murgatroyd and Morgan's (1993) model. They define 'commitment' as team support for the achievement of shared goals, 'communication' as being a free-flowing, open, simple and effective interchange of views, and 'culture' as being one in which innovation is highly valued.

Conclusions

The need for schools to take on more complex managerial responsibility and become more accountable due to the education reforms of the 1980s, the emergence of the market, and the need for self-evaluation and improvement planning which increasingly occupies school managers' thoughts since the launch of the OFSTED inspection system, have required the emergence of more sophisticated management strategies focused on the delivery of a quality service based upon client need. Thus schools are aware of the need to adapt more traditional bureaucratic/autocratic management practices to cope with the customer-driven market economy. It is clear that effective school management, which depends heavily on the impetus of the head teacher and senior management team in sharing and conveying a sense of vision and purpose for the school, implies the adoption of strategies and tools which, through the empowerment of work teams, will enable the school to move continuously towards the fulfilment of clear, customer-focused goals, regularly reviewing and evaluating quality against appropriate performance criteria. The effectively managed school appears to be one which regards itself as a learning organisation for all its members, in that, far from seeking to maintain and replicate existing levels of quality and performance, it adopts a questioning and self-critical stance in a search for 'Kaizen', the Japanese philosophy of 'continuous improvement'. This is closely related to the work of the 'quality gurus' such as Deming, Juran and Crosby, and which is at the heart of the concept of 'total quality management'. The evidence suggests that the adoption of the Management

Review and Improvement system, based on a framework of standards or benchmarks capable of defining the functions of school management and suggesting criteria for competent performance, provided a valuable tool to set the participant schools on the road to 'Kaizen', and hence to quality management.

ANNEX 1

STANDARDS FOR SCHOOL MANAGEMENT

An overview of the Key Purpose, Key Roles and Units of
Competence for School Management

Key Purpose

Create, maintain, review and develop the conditions which enable
teachers and pupils to achieve effective learning.

Key Roles or Functions	*Units of Competence*
A *Manage Policy*	**A1** Review, develop and present school aims, policies and objectives.
	A2 Develop supportive relationships with pupils, staff, parents, governors and the community.
B *Manage Learning*	**B1** Review, develop and implement means for supporting pupils' learning.
	B2 Monitor and evaluate learning programme.
C *Manage People*	**C1** Recruit and select teaching and non-teaching staff.
	C2 Develop teams, individuals and self to enhance performance.
	C3 Plan, allocate and evaluate work carried out by teams, individuals and self.
	C4 Create, maintain and enhance effective working relationships.
D *Manage Resources*	**D1** Secure effective resource allocation.
	D2 Monitor and control the use of resources.

Source: Earley (1992b) *The School Management Competences Project: Standards for School Management.* Crawley: School
Management South.

ANNEX 2

MANAGEMENT REVIEW AND IMPROVEMENT WORKSHOPS
QUESTIONNAIRE A

Participants were asked to respond to each statement on a scale of 5 (strongly agree) to 1 (strongly disagree)

1. The involvement of an external facilitator had a positive effect on the way we worked as a team.

2. The workshops increased our knowledge and understanding of the tasks involved in managing the school.

3. The workshops gave us a clearer understanding of the management tasks involved in our own individual roles.

4. The workshops had a positive effect on the team's confidence in its ability to manage the school effectively.

5. The workshops enabled useful links to be made between Standards for School Management and the OFSTED Inspection Framework.

6. The workshops helped us to identify improvement needs and set realistic goals.

7. Completing Record of Management Review sheets increased our sense of progress and achievement.

8. Using Standards for School Management made the review process logical and straightforward.

9. Using Standards for School Management as a tool for review and improvement is likely to enhance the long-term management effectiveness of the team.

10. Using the Management Review and Improvement process has already shown the potential to make a positive impact on the management of teaching and learning in this school.

ANNEX 3

MANAGEMENT REVIEW AND IMPROVEMENT WORKSHOPS
QUESTIONNAIRE B

On a scale of 5 (high) to 1 (low), participants were asked to rate the impact of the workshops in reinforcing their ability to display each of the following characteristics of effective teams

1. Showing drive and a sense of purpose.

2. Showing a commitment to development.

3. Willingness to adopt a self-critical and self-evaluative approach to school improvement.

4. Ability to formulate clear objectives and means of achieving them.

5. A positive attitude to identifying problems and seeking solutions.

6. Flexibility in coping with change.

7. Having and articulating shared values and beliefs.

8. Shared decision-making and consensus seeking.

9. Willingness to participate in discussion.

10. Willingness to take action and make things happen.

11. Ability to communicate effectively with each other in an open and honest way.

12. Willingness to approach tasks co-operatively and collaboratively.

13. Willingness to listen to each other and value each other's contribution.

14. Seeking to recognise and make the best use of the qualities and experiences of each team member.

15. A sense of enjoyment and satisfaction in working together as a team.

CHAPTER EIGHT

'Investors in People': A Consultant's View

by Nick Zienau

This chapter is based on the experience of a project involving more than 40 schools in South East London working with a team of six consultants. It is written from the point of view of a consultant by which is meant that person outside the school who assists the school to develop – the external change agent – considered by Fullan to be a necessary component of educational change (Fullan 1982). In this sense employees of various agencies, local authority advisers, school inspectors, school managers active in schools other than their own and colleagues from Higher Education who are involved in school improvement may all be said to be 'consultants'.

The goal of writing has been to be specific about the rationale for using the 'Investors in People' standard in school development or improvement, to share our experience of doing it in a fairly general way and to draw together our learning and the issues that have been raised in this work. Our proposition is that 'Investors in People' should be taken seriously as a tool for use in school improvement programmes. In our view 'Investors in People' is important because it is an effective method of bringing a school's internal processes to a consistent standard which will assist greatly in achieving quality of teaching and learning and without which little lasting improvement is possible.

What is 'Investors in People' and what can it do?

'Investors in People' was originally developed as a list of organisational standards or indicators to encourage employers to increase their commitment to train and develop their workforce. This was part of an effort by government in the United Kingdom undertaken by the National Training Task Force. 'Investors' was launched as a national standard in November

1990. Achieving the Standard in a specified proportion of organisations is currently part of the National Education and Training Targets, which include as part of the goal of lifetime learning that by the year 2000: '70 per cent of all organisations employing 200 or more employees, and 35 per cent of those employing 50 or more to be recognised as Investors in People' (NACETT 1994).

These targets are supported by many organisations including: the Secondary Heads Association, Trades Union Congress, National Association of Head Teachers, Equal Opportunities Commission as well as the Confederation of British Industry and OFSTED. In that sense one can see the Standard as representing an interesting social contract between a number of significant forces affecting British education at least at the formal level.

Through Training and Enterprise Councils (TECs) the government is financially supporting organisations of all types to achieve the Standard which is a benchmark of good practice in employee development and quality through people-oriented management. It consists of a profile bank of 24 statements or indicators which are used as a way of diagnosing and responding to deficiencies in the infrastructure of management practice within an organisation. (The indicators are reproduced in the Appendix to this book.)

As working consultants in an era of locally managed and financed schools we have found this important and helpful for a number of reasons:

- funding is available to subsidise work in school;
- the Standard demands of us that we help leadership in the school examine the reality of life within the organisation they lead;
- discipline and a structure is helpful to school staff and to making clear the consultant's objectives and success criteria;
- external assessment which requires systematic implementation and consistency.

The method

A set of statements about organisational effectiveness are used (the indicators) to diagnose and analyse procedural and interpersonal functions necessary for the learning and development process within the school to work effectively. The process starts by making sure that the leadership of the school see in the indicators a useful set of conditions and attributes that are worth achieving. Generally we have found that people readily accept the values underlying these statements as desirable for the school whatever their position in the structure. People rarely argue about the value of any of the indicators. Scepticism is more often expressed toward the origin of the Standard in industry and the value of its transfer to schools.

Once ownership of the Standard as a worthwhile goal has been established, data gathering by the consultant and/or by internal personnel can begin. The diagnosis is followed by joint work to create an Action Plan by the consultant and the school, after which an implementation project can be designed and integrated with other elements of the school's Development Plan.

Generally the items addressed by the diagnosis will be concerned with changes in the process which underlie the school's work and will therefore sit alongside the plans for improvement in the school's performance in relation to pupils' learning in the same way as building works and other capital investments would. It is our experience that in the most successful cases achieving 'Investors in People' becomes one of the goals of the Plan alongside other output related objectives during the implementation of the project.

The project's implementation may or may not involve external help and typically takes a year or more to complete. The process of assessment and accreditation by independent assessors usually follows, which, when successful, results in the school being formally recognised as an 'Investor in People'.

Having a distinctive approach as a consultancy to the 'Investors in People' process has been important to motivate us and inform the way we implement it. Central to our thinking has been the idea that the value system and skill of consultants employed in the work is as important to people in school as the validity of the instrument. Our starting point is that the way we help the school and the methodology we use have probably as much impact as the end product. We have always believed in telling staff of the school that the Standard usually demands some degree of cultural change. In turn we explain that we are prepared to help schools deal with difficulties and resistance to the changes implied by the Standard in a skilful, informed and sympathetic way. We know this includes facing the fact that some of this resistance will be acted out toward the consultant. We have learnt how useful it can be to reflect this back to the client in appropriate ways as a dynamic means of diagnosing and making clear the problems that the school faces. At a very trivial level it means that when consulting in a school we immediately experience whether meetings start on time, how people relate to authority, how open people are with each other and so on. By feeding this information back appropriately we can add greatly to the understanding of the whole school community around the problem of change and improvement in the school.

Schools rightly expect consultants to give clear guidance about methods of diagnosis, time to become involved and the likely value of such an exercise as a priority in relation to other approaches to promoting school effectiveness. It is our goal to be as expert in such matters as we can and to take responsibility for continually learning which methodology to apply to particular school conditions.

Impact on schools – achievement and accountability

When schools have a culture of low expectations of pupils this often seems to be reflected in the quality of professional communication apparent between school managers and staff, and in the dialogue in the staff room. By pointing out in a diagnosis the way that low expectations appears as a cultural issue affecting the whole school, we can begin to point out that low expectations do not just involve children, but can also be dealt with directly by teachers having a higher expectation of each other. Our experience draws us to believe that in the same way as a hologram can be broken in half so can a culture be seen in small parts of the whole social organisation. We therefore work from a belief that by altering the culture among teachers it is possible to affect the cultural stance toward pupils indirectly.

Schools which are fairly effective but wish to improve or upgrade their current management methods and practices can also benefit. These schools tend to use the Standard as a means of diagnosing their problem in a way that is referenced to 'good practice' and avoid quick fixes that patch up management practices rather than improve them systematically. In that sense the Standard also becomes a basic curriculum for managers to follow which covers the main aspects of the managers job in relation to his or her most difficult and important task of managing staff.

All schools in England and Wales have had in the last few years to accept an increased level of formal accountability through external inspection and a national curriculum. This, combined with greater school autonomy through site-based management of resources, is placing managers in a position where they must justify the decisions they make and where the consequences become more visible than formerly was the case. One consequence of this change in national priorities has been several years in which schools have tended to adopt top-down management practice to keep up with mandated requirements. These include changes in the curriculum and increased formal accountability for school output measures. A frequent consequence of this in many of the schools in which we work has been the perceived dis-empowerment of 'middle managers' who were used to having a lot of autonomy and freedom to decide how far to control the content and style of their work and that of their unit or department.

One of the needs commonly expressed in schools we work with is for middle management training. Senior managers are concerned about the distance between them and their middle management colleagues, while knowing that quality improvement relies heavily on the adequate work of the middle management stratum.

Having a framework of statements helps us contextualise such a need and view the school as a system and a working community. It also allows us to fix those issues or changes that are necessary in senior management practice without which there can be no real improvement in management processes. As one head said to us after we had worked in his school: 'Now I really feel a confidence that we are taking the whole picture into account and not simply trying to fix the one hole in the roof that the rain is coming through at the moment'.

We build on the concept of collegiality and co-operation throughout the school by clarifying and defining the managerial role at different levels.

The need for adult learning

The schools we are working with comprise a range of secondary, primary, nursery and special schools. The Standard's statements help define processes which are necessary for learning to take place among adults in the whole school community. A strong merit of the method that we have found in most schools has been that it empowers schools to use the talent and expertise they already have to better effect. It includes support staff as equally important partners in expertise and talent. We prefer this to approaches which start from the assumption that external specialist knowledge or expertise about teaching is automatically required for improvement of quality to take place.

Although most of our team of consultants have an educational background, we come into the school in the first place from the position that the school probably has much of the necessary expertise and human capital needed to improve. In the first place our role is to start helping free the ways in which that potential can be fully realised.

Key issues identified in schools

Key elements of school management practice which are illuminated by this process include:

- Effectiveness of senior managers' efforts to:
  - Define and clarify managerial roles and functions in the school and define working teams
  - Define a method for clear decision-making around development issues in the school
  - Create a framework which enables staff at all levels to own and contribute to development plans.

- Team leaders and middle managers work to:
  - Create accountability among staff for unit performance in achieving school objectives
  - Manage people within their unit by appropriate support and challenge
  - Facilitate staff development in groups and at individual level.

- Non-teaching staff development which means:
  - Appropriate management and team structures which involve them as full contributors to the effectiveness of the school
  - Creating appropriate staff development provision within the school to support their learning
  - Access to resources for training and development.

- Forming and organising teams which:
  - Focus on quality improvement in the classroom
  - Provide adequate space for professional debate, reflection and development
  - Help people develop the skills to improve teaching
  - Create the best environment for learning in the school.

Initial findings

Four conclusions emanated from our first year's work.

1. We think we have evidence that the 'Investors in People' framework helps to create conditions in which a systematic attempt at developing the organisation is effective because it creates workable boundaries for consultants and schools to work within. Concretely this means that there is always a clear and meaningful task to do in meeting the criteria which the 24 statements create. In our experience the most difficult part of projects which aim to change organisations in general and schools in particular is maintaining the commitment and the clarity of task. This is particularly the case when obstacles, inertia or temporary halts due to normal operating conditions of the school take attention away from the long-term goal of organisational change.
2. There is wide acceptance of the idea that infrastructure development is necessary before effective development is possible among managers, teachers and others involved in the project. People have begun

118

to see why previous improvement efforts have come to a halt because the root causes in the school culture were not addressed. This is also confirmed by researchers such as Fullan who has shown how innovation and improvement in schools is thwarted by implementation problems which are not addressed (Fullan 1991).

3. That at least in the situation in London it may become a good focus around which collaboration amongst schools can be created. At a time of competition and autonomy of schools, it focuses on a common theme which can unite the professional community in education. There is a clear common goal of creating good professional conditions for all who work in education which 'Investors in People' can be used to address. Many school leaders recognise how important it is to create a well qualified pool of capable staff and wish to ensure they are doing their part to contribute to this in schools. They find it easy to co-operate in systematic work to make this happen. We also believe this is a good opportunity for school leaders to network and share good practice around management issues in practical ways which they value.

4. That the idea of a Standard which can define effective management practice is a good one – particularly when the criteria are the thoughts, perceptions and experiences of those who work in schools and not simply 'procedures on paper'. All assessment and diagnosis is on the basic assumption that development of staff depends on reality as perceived by those being developed and not simply on paper systems. The use of the Standard therefore encourages consultants and management groups to address the issues that affect motivation and performance which are the actual thoughts and feelings of those who make the school work.

Issues for consultants and advisers

This section is meant to be useful to teams of advisers/consultants who attempt to set up similar projects and it should also give school managers some insight into what they might ask of their consultants.

Our professional starting point was process-based and we were sympathetic to the 'Organisation Development' school of Per Dalin and colleagues (Dalin and Rolff 1993). The underlying logic of this approach is that consultants need to work not simply at an expert level of offering advice about changes and innovations about which they have knowledge and expertise. Rather they have to see themselves as the facilitators of the change process in the school itself and act to enable the school to change itself. Such Organisation Development (OD) processes are slow and it is often hard to keep the work focused on achievable objectives that mean something in the reality of school life. This is a problem that has to be solved when time and costs of development have to be met from the school's own training budget. 'Investors in People' indicators have proved to be useful and concrete enough to act as real objectives for the kind of OD work that Dalin considers useful. They have the additional advantage of a nationally organised assessment system with a system of external validation and accreditation.

The method of working uses the Standard's 24 statements as the goal to achieve and suggests a four phase process with the following stages:

- diagnosis/gap analysis
- action plan
- implementation
- assessment.

Our comments refer to the first three phases.

Phase 1: Diagnosis

Diagnosis helps to structure a clear 'management curriculum' for schools in which there is often little common understanding across the staff of what function managers/leaders are actually there to perform. The statements form the basic themes and become an aid to working out what that 'curriculum' will be in that particular school. The process acts as a stimulus to clarify the basic managerial values that a school has at present or wishes to adopt for the future. As consultants we strive to help schools to bring their managerial values into alignment with their pedagogical ones.

Making good diagnostic reports and statements based on the subjective experience of members of staff is an exacting one. Consultants and school leaders have to take care when interpreting the data and not jump hastily to conclusions about what it means. For example, staff may report that their experience of being inducted was not satisfactory as an introduction to their work. This does not mean that existing teachers 'don't give a damn about their new colleagues'. Of course it may do, but it is also possible that they simply have fixed on other priorities in the hustle of school life. For us the important step to take is that senior managers begin to look at this fact, think about its impact on the school and the staff, and think with us about what might be done to 'close the gap' between the indicator and the reality we have found in the experiences of the staff. This includes thinking about how important the gap is and what are the priorities for action among those in management positions.

Whatever the diagnosis, it is important that the senior figures in the school recognise and own the results. Often such ownership comes about by ensuring that difficult issues are not dodged, that the diagnosis has used a number of data gathering methods in order to fix key points which people recognise as accurate, and that detailed and convincing evidence is given of the fairness and integrity of the process. For instance, our practice has generally been to combine questionnaires and formal data gathering with semi-structured interviews and group interviews.

The professional and independent view of the consultant is in our experience an important ingredient in legitimising the diagnosis in the eyes of the school community. This status has to be won by demonstration. Often the consultant's presence is also important to allow a full dialogue to take place between colleagues in the school about the results. It often seems the case that this is the most important result of the diagnostic feedback. Senior people are enabled to get to grips with issues they have thought about for years, known were important to the functioning of the school, but have hitherto not discussed because the focus was not created. The advantage of having clear criteria is that they allow the discussion to be depersonalised and focused on needs and functions rather than personalities. Almost all heads and senior staff have reported that they find this helpful.

Phase 2: Action Plans

This phase of the assignment is usually undertaken as a close continuation of the diagnosis and is then carried forward as a living example of 'live planning'. Periodically it is referred to, modified, extended as a guide to understanding implementation timing and responsibilities. The Action Plan is the plan of the school, but our finding in practice is that many schools appreciate the help of consultants in working out the best way to respond to gaps. It seems that help in managing the change and development process at organisational level is appreciated by schools because they may lack the full range of expertise in managing change. Consultants who choose to work on an organisational change programme like 'Investors in People' can assist schools by being expert in the research literature, techniques and case studies of school development. We have also found that schools appreciate a 'systems approach' from the consultant which helps them see how different parts of the whole school fit together and interact. Consultants need to be expert enough to advise school leaders on the options they have for implementation and action, and learn from contact with a wide experimental base of change efforts.

Phase 3: Implementation

There seem to us to be two basic hypotheses that one can take about

'Investors in People' in schools. The choice of hypothesis determines quite different approaches to implementation of changes.

> *Hypothesis 1 Schools need gaps in their practice to be pointed out to them. Once that is done or they have done this for themselves it is then possible for them (or individuals within the school) methodically to make the changes that are required to fix the gaps or obtain the concrete help they need to do so.*

If we wanted to give this a name we might say that it is a *rational model* based on the assumption that people have the fundamental ability to be sensible about what is going on and mobilise their energies to the task of changing it.

> *Hypothesis 2 People in schools normally know (more or less) the kind of conclusions that are likely to come up in an 'Investors in People' diagnosis or gap analysis. Mostly they have known these things for a long time, but felt unable to do anything to alter the situation or felt that it was not so important as other priorities. There may be considerable doubt about whether there is any real action that can be taken that will change the situation because of people, personalities, the history of the school and so on.*

I would describe this second hypothesis as having an *existential* element in which things seem beyond the scope of human intervention or even understanding. Forces seem to prevent otherwise sensible human beings taking fairly obvious steps to fill functional gaps that are fairly apparent to the average observer.

In actual practice with 'Investors in People' casework we find considerable evidence of this second hypothesis holding good *at least to some extent*. It may be part of the mental map that people create of an institution – a sort of assumption that this is just how it is in this particular school and nothing that anyone will do can change it – our tendency to collude with our own sense of powerlessness.

Increasingly we are drawn to the belief that in most schools it will be helpful to assume that some hypothesis 2 phenomena will occur during implementation and in particular will occur when 'difficult' interpersonal or cultural changes are attempted. For this reason it is our practice to explain that this is a part of the process that the school is undertaking. We also try to make clear in our contract with schools that we have a function in helping understand the 'irrational' side of the organisational change process. We think that by doing this we also help schools to make informed choices about their own change programmes and avoid predictable failures and disappointment.

Implications for consultants are that schools are likely to need help in the implementation phase that goes beyond informational material, seminars on how to fulfil the criteria of assessment, or the installation of new systems. These only suffice when hypothesis 1 holds good. If hypothesis 2 is valid then help is required with the process of organisational learning including the issue of resistance and the 'process' issues named by Schein (1988) and Block (1981).

For this consultants need courage, training and *a conviction that their efforts make a unique contribution to the process of change in the school*. This conviction will of course begin to be shared by an increasing number of members of the school working community through experience when the consultant's work begins to make a real impact on the life of the school. If not – then he/she is in trouble unless the failure to be effective is recognised at an early stage so the reasons for this can be discussed with the client and solutions found.

In order to deal with this hypothesis 2 world our approach to implementation has evolved to include the following five principles:

- A clear contract with the school of the intention to deal with blocks to implementation wherever they occur.
- An emphasis on the use and development of internal capacity to handle and develop the concrete issues of management and development in-school.
- Linking 'Investors in People' to the vision of the future of the school (especially a vision of a professional community for all staff).
- Integrating with other internal change processes and programmes to simplify rather than complicate strategic management of the school.
- A clear link with the fundamental goals and aims of the school (e.g. 'Investors in People' as a means by which the school will deliver better differentiation rather than an end in itself).

Development of effective consultants

It is our belief that discipline and skill are the essentials that consultants must possess. We have no doubt from the reaction of our clients to this approach that all agencies working in school advice and improvement will have to pay more attention to these skills in future. As those in the front line of education – the schools – obtain an increasing say over the services and support that they receive from outside agencies, we see a necessity to make those services client-focused and therefore effective in helping implement real changes. In this we would include local and national government, universities and teacher training institutions and consultancies like our own.

In our own work in the field and in running seminars with other school consultants and advisers, we conceptualise effective consulting as requiring the following elements:

- Expertise and ability to hold authority in a field or method.
- Consulting skills to manage the relationship and the assignment with the client.
- Understanding of the organisational context and dynamics of change in schools.
- Clear commitment to ethical behaviour and authenticity in relationships.

In our practice this begins to form a framework for understanding our professionality and what membership of a professional community in consulting might mean in the future. The shift in our concept of the role of the consultant is from subject expert to skilled practitioner. In fact both are necessary. This bears a strong relationship to the shift in schools from a focus on subject and curriculum knowledge of teachers (the knowledgeable practitioner) to a focus on student learning and a self-critical approach to the behaviour and actions of one's own practice in teaching (the reflective and skilled practitioner). As we go on with this project we are, as consultants, trying to become professionally self-critical. Part of our aim is also to enable schools to develop a culture in which adults can be professionally self-critical about the actions they take to help their students and children learn.

CHAPTER NINE

Achieving School Improvement through 'Investors in People': Perspectives from the Primary Sector

by Marie Brown, John Taylor and Roger Whittaker

'Investors in People' is an award of public recognition achieved by companies who pursue business success through the continuous development of their management and staff. It aims to help businesses improve their performance by realising the full potential of their staff and is based on the experience of many successful UK companies. This amalgam of good practice has demonstrated that performance is improved by a planned approach to:

> *setting and communicating business goals*
> and
> *developing people to meet these goals*
> so that *what people can do and are motivated to do, matches what the business needs them to do.*

The basis of 'Investors in People' is a national Standard which provides indicators to which an organisation can work and a benchmark against which progress can be measured (see the Appendix to this book). Once organisations are assessed as having met this Standard, they can be publicly recognised as an 'Investor in People'. Whilst the achievement of the Award provides benefits in the eyes of potential recruits, current employees and not least customers, the real benefits are brought about by the journey to meet the indicators and the increasing involvement and contribution from the workforce at all levels. An organisation's involvement will only be effective if the belief in achieving the aims of 'Investors in People' comes from its very top.

Getting started

The first step on the 'Investor's' journey is to find out how strong the school's commitment is to people. A survey of a cross-section of management and staff, with questions based on the 'Investors' Standard and tailored to the level of employee, will give an indication as to how committed the school is and what may remain to be done.

Having established this, an Action Plan is developed, showing clearly the steps to be taken, by whom and when. The speed of the journey is determined by the school in the light of how much there is to do and the operational constraints of the School Development Plan. The benefits to the school arise from the achievement of the Award and the recognition that it has achieved the Standard.

There are four stages in the journey:

– Commitment
– Planning
– Action
– Evaluation

Commitment An 'Investor in People' makes a public commitment from the top to develop all employees. A letter of commitment is sent by the head teacher to the school's local Training and Enterprise Council (TEC). It is necessary to ensure that the school has a flexible plan which sets goals and targets, stating how employees will contribute and how development needs will be met. It communicates to all employees where the organisation is going and the contribution they will make.

Planning An 'Investor in People' reviews the training and development needs of all its employees and identifies these in the Business Plan, agreeing individual needs with each employee.

Action An 'Investor in People' takes action to train and develop individuals, from recruitment and throughout their employment, and encourages all employees to contribute to their own job-related needs.

Evaluation This is usually the most difficult stage for any organisation. A continuous assessment of the competence and commitment of all employees is made against business goals/targets and the effectiveness of training in meeting these established. Importantly, as goals/targets change, the effectiveness of the workforce to meet these future needs is reviewed.

What are the benefits?

'Investing in People' adds teeth to quality programmes which may already be in existence. Real benefits to an 'Investor in People' school can be expected in:

- Improved performance
- Increased personnel motivation, commitment and loyalty
- Greater customer satisfaction
- Organisational reputation

An increasing number of primary and secondary schools of all types and sizes are choosing to become 'Investors in People'. Whilst they will be seen as high quality organisations, the real benefit experienced is in their operational performance. The following is an account of consultancy and training work for 'Investors' in a cluster of Staffordshire primary schools, undertaken by staff from the University of Manchester, together with the personal views of one of the primary head teachers on the process.

'Investors' in Staffordshire primary schools

In the School of Education of the University of Manchester, there has been a high level of primary school involvement in courses designed to help schools improve the quality of their provision. These have ranged from those concerned with updating on the National Curriculum and its attendant legislation, to those concerned with issues of management, parental involvement and preparation for OFSTED. Primary schools have been in the forefront of this course expansion and it is possible to see a change in the schools involved. They feel the need to look with more precision at the quality of what they provide and the learning outcomes for children.

About 18 months ago, a number of primary schools in Staffordshire became involved with the School of Education in an 'Investors' project. They attended a one day course designed to inform primary school senior managers about the implications of OFSTED inspection. Follow-up consultancy was offered during the course, and this included 'Investors in People' as a means of helping schools along the route to quality improvement, and therefore an aid for schools facing inspection. We were, at that stage, careful to say that 'Investors in People' would prove very helpful to schools in putting quality processes in place. Although this would assist in improving management methods, it would not deal directly with curriculum issues or the quality of teaching and learning.

The next step was a meeting with the schools in their cluster (six primary schools and one special school) in order to explore further what would be involved. This included sharing with them the essentials of the 'Investors' model. They clearly had a desire to work towards the long-term quality improvement which is the hallmark of the process and were, at this stage, content that curriculum issues could be addressed later through the expertise of the consultants. At this stage, OFSTED was treated as one element of the current situation in which schools found themselves. They also knew that they could call on further time and expertise to focus on OFSTED if they wished to do so at any point in the process.

'Investors' processes

The process for each school commenced with an audit of the current position with respect to the Standard, and the preparation of an Action Plan. It was important to meet with all staff – teachers and support staff – in each school in order to outline the process, assure them that it was not an 'inspection in disguise' and enlist their support for completion of a staff questionnaire. It proved most valuable, whenever this was possible, to meet with governors and brief them fully. Consultants spent some two hours meeting with heads and deputies and chairs of governors in order to elicit current management methods and processes. This provided the additional benefit of enabling the consultant to introduce the principles of 'Investors' and the good practice that would help to achieve the Standard. Armed with the audit evidence of management methods and processes, staff questionnaire analysis and documentation, consultants prepared the Action Plans and fed these back to heads, deputies and chairs of governors. It proved very beneficial to brief a wider audience of staff and, in one school, parents also.

All the schools then moved on to the second phase of the programme, which consisted of training and consultancy to assist in achieving the Standard. The aims of the training were:

- to familiarise course members with the Standard and its principles and requirements;
- to clarify the good practice which enables the components of the Standard to be achieved;
- to equip course members to assess the progress being made towards the Standard in their own schools.

The training programme itself consisted of a series of one day sessions as follows:

1. *'Investors' awareness* – focusing on the 24 indicators and their inter-pretation in the context of schools, how a judgement is reached, the role of the assessor and overview of the key management processes.

2. *Identifying staff development needs* – focusing on appraisal culture, school needs and individual needs, target-setting, role of the line man-ager, training needs analysis, coaching and counselling, quality processes including appraisal skills, the appraisal process for support staff, what the assessor will look for.

3. *The evidence* – focusing on what the assessor will look for to see that systems are in place, preparing the portfolio, links with OFSTED, policy statements and schemes of work, preparation of a staff devel-opment policy.

4. *Planning processes* – focusing on strategic planning, school develop-ment planning, action planning, SWOT analysis, quality processes.

5. *Communications processes* – focusing on involvement of all staff, induction, staff handbook, leadership styles and management methods, the central importance of staff perceptions, what the assessor will look for.

6. *Evaluation processes* – focusing on methods of evaluation, perfor-mance measurement, organisational review, individual review, recognising quality improvements, what the assessor will look for.

7. *Preparing for Assessment* – focusing on collecting the evidence, preparing the storyboard, pre-assessment checks, what to expect, the assessment.

Training for 'Investors'

The training sessions were held over a seven month period and were attended by heads and deputies from each school. The focus of the train-ing sessions was determined in part by the requirements of 'Investors', but also by the needs identified by the schools. The emphases within the sessions, therefore, became the property of the schools. One particular case was the schools' belief that teacher appraisal was not operating effectively for the staff concerned, nor in terms of the schools' need for clear targeting of work and clarity of staff development. Time was spent on this issue in order that appraisal could be rethought, and relaunched where necessary, thus giving schools more confidence in the process. It was also necessary to clarify the approach needed for non-teaching staff so that a scheme in line with 'Investors' principles could be put in place. Useful inputs to sessions came from the Total Quality Management approach, which is taught within the University as a module on the M.Ed. in Educational Management and Administration. These underpinned the training dealing with the aspects of good practice needed to implement 'Investors' effectively. From the perspective of the consultants, a great deal was gained from the interaction and collaborative working done by the schools during the training programme. Shared understandings of how to implement processes, or build on present practice were a feature of the training sessions. It underlined the fact that schools were not in competition but were striving towards a common goal – high quality education for all the children in the schools.

'Investors' consultancy

In-school consultancy followed on from the training. The main purpose was to help schools determine whether they were effective in implementation. At this stage the consultants acted as assessors. It was quite clear that the decision to provide heads and deputies with the perspectives of the assessor for each of the training sessions had paid off. Schools were quite clear about how far key features of 'Investors' were progressing and therefore wanted the consultant to double check. This was very valuable both to schools and to consultants in that it enabled the 'health check' to be conducted at a level where quality discussion about mutually understood issues could start immediately.

The pre-assessment (health check) was looked at in two ways: in terms of the portfolio and storyboard, and in terms of the perceptions of staff. The storyboard, provision of documentary evidence that all of the 24 indicators are being met, was the most straightforward process. The words can be fine-tuned and revisions made and the in-depth knowledge of the consultant about the school can be brought to bear on the storyboard. Discovering the attitudes of staff towards 'Investors' is most critical. Part of the assessment process is the finding of evidence from staff that the principles of 'Investors' are understood and working. Where time allowed, all staff were seen, and where not, a cross-section was chosen. The views of staff testified to the power of the process and some key generalisations can be made:

1. Support staff feel, sometimes for the first time, that they are genuinely part of a wider team and not the 'also rans'.

2. All staff feel that they are fully involved in the planning processes of the school whether their work lies within the classroom or outside it.

3. Support staff feel that they understand the goals and direction of the school, understand where they make their contribution and feel highly

valued – so much so that in many cases they want to give the school '110 per cent'.

4. All staff feel that they have greater clarity about what is expected of them, have clear work targets which match the School Development Plan and have their training needs identified and met wherever possible.

5. Staff feel that the schools have a different culture now, one of greater cohesion, greater staff involvement, a climate of staff empowerment, better planning, clarity of work targets, better targeted staff development, greater readiness to make changes – in fact, generally a better place to work.

6. Staff value the managerial reviews/appraisals which help to clarify their work targets and agree staff development needs. Some of the old suspicions about appraisal are no longer present.

7. Some staff feel that one of their initial concerns that 'Investors' sounded like a management-led exercise which would not prove of value to them have been completely dispelled.

8. Staff feel that 'management' has been quite brave to make all these changes but are also delighted by the outcomes.

In general, staff sense that they have been enabled to succeed and work to best effect. Consultants have asked teaching staff if they perceive that the quality of the education provided for children has improved. In general the answer is 'yes', but it is interesting that they consider that this particular issue needs to be checked out, measured and understood on the basis of facts, not just impressions. Some staff feel that the way forward now is for them to be trained in the techniques of assessment of quality in teaching and learning and how to use these in their work. Going through the 'Investors' procedures has motivated staff to follow a route to continuous quality improvement. It may have started as a management inspired exercise, but the evidence from the Staffordshire schools suggests that it is now being increasingly driven by staff.

A personal view from a primary head teacher

The following is the personal view of a primary school head teacher, Roger Whittaker from Staffordshire, whose school was the first in the county to gain the 'Investors in People' award.

The school started on the 'Investors' trail in January 1994. It was, at that time, perceived as a user-friendly means of checking certain

OFSTED processes prior to an inspection. Certainly, the process would look closely at the management of the school, the documentation that was in place and the training and development of the staff. These being relevant areas that OFSTED would want to look at, 'Investors', I felt, was a positive move on our part to pre-empt OFSTED and ensure certain vital principles were in place.

The 'Investors' programme would not look at classroom practice

This was not seen as a problem because at this stage it was important not to put the teaching staff under pressure, and the manner of introducing 'Investors' would not do this. Their involvement, as with the support staff, would be at a level they could feel comfortable with; more especially, they could see the relevance of 'Investors' in helping them in their role in school, particularly in relation to their training and development. It followed from this premise that if we were looking critically at the management of the school there would be positive benefits for the staff and their development. Effective management creates the climate for good working relationships and practices. This could in turn improve the quality of delivery in the classroom by the teaching staff and have a more positive effect on the work delivered by the support staff. It soon became clear that, while 'Investors' could be looked at as pre-OFSTED preparation, it was much more than that.

'Investors' became a culture within school

It developed merit within its own right and the relationship with OFSTED became insignificant. It absorbed our thinking, especially when looking at the development of people. I thought I knew my colleagues, but through 'Investors' and the practices we have put into place, I now know them a lot better. This has been brought about through the introduction of my Professional Development Discussions with all staff, my appraisal of them and their roles in school, their aims and ambitions for themselves, their development needs to meet these ambitions and their targets for the future. Everybody suddenly now had a personal development plan which dovetailed into the overall School Development Plan. This certainly created a stronger sense of worth and belonging, especially for the support staff.

There has been a greater sense of unity within the school. The teaching staff have become more aware of the role of the support staff especially as this has been more clearly defined. This has resulted in better interaction between all staff and a greater appreciation of each others' roles. The impact on the support staff has been most noticeable. Training opportunities were developed by the school for them, where before no training had been provided. For example, a package of training for lunchtime supervisors evolved through their Development Discussions which included aspects of child play, managing children, health and safety and first aid. Training packages initiated by the school for personal welfare assistants, caretakers, janitors and receptionists have all been delivered this year.

The necessity for this training saw a further development in the liaison between the cluster schools. To become economic, the training costs needed to be shared and not focused on one school. It was apparent that all the cluster schools had common elements of development needs for their support staffs, so it was easy to share training and hence rationalise costs.

'Investors' has been a catalyst in the strengthening of cluster relationships

The shared training opportunities for support staff have now similarly developed for the teaching staff. Areas of common need have been identified and trainers bought in to deliver within the cluster of schools. The year has seen the development of 'Whole Partnership Planning' and staff training and development has formed a part of this. Through 'Investors' the partnership has evolved joint policies, especially in the more controversial areas of admissions, exclusions, lettings and sex education, which again has strengthened the union between the schools. The benefits have not just been in the area of cost-effectiveness, but in developing relationships between the personnel within the schools. Opportunities to share ideas and practices, discuss problems and celebrate successes have arisen.

'Investors' has further united and strengthened the personnel within our partnership of schools

I mentioned earlier that one of the aspects 'Investors' looked at was the documentation within the school. This has led to the development of uniform policy statements for curriculum and general school activities. The advent of a Handbook which was user-friendly for all staff was most significant. The drafting of the School Development Plan took on a different form with all staff having an opportunity to make a contribution.

'Investors' has developed a stronger community within our school

During the year of our involvement in 'Investors' we have come a long way as a school. Changes in attitudes, the development of people, the strengthening of our community and the enhancement of planning and communications have all been in evidence. During the year the partnership of cluster schools has strengthened because of our mutual commitment to 'Investors'.

'Investors' was the necessary catalyst to set all this in motion

It has all been achieved because of a desire on everyone's part, both in school and within the cluster, to develop with the aim of bettering our schools and the community we each serve. The area that is more difficult to judge, one year on, is to assess whether 'Investors' has had any impact on the teaching and learning within school. Certainly relationships between those support staff who come into contact with children have been enhanced by the training and development they have received. They feel more confident and so more able to perform well in their jobs. I would like to think that by extending the school's appraisal process into one where an individual's own training and development is the central focus and ensuring that quality training follows, then the quality of teaching and learning in the classroom should be enhanced.

'Performance' is improved in the classroom

If through 'Investors' a person feels more valued and that their training is more focused, then it should follow that their performance is improved in the classroom. I have no real evidence to support this at the present time. However, it is an area that will be addressed because classroom management and practice is our school's focus in the School Development Plan. This particular focus comes as a result of staff initiative and follows directly from the 'Investors' emphasis this year on management and personal development.

CHAPTER TEN

A Comprehensive School's Experience of Working Towards 'Investors in People'

by Peter Thomas

This chapter provides a critical assessment of the possibility of achieving school improvement through working towards the national Standard 'Investors in People' (IiP). It reflects on the experiences at one comprehensive school which has been working towards achieving the national Standard for the last two years.

How commitment to 'Investors' was made

Following a series of courses on quality and performance management attended by the head teacher and deputies early in 1993, the senior management team (SMT) resolved to set about improving quality management across the school. The SMT came to the view that existing approaches were largely ad hoc and incremental and had to be overhauled. To provide a unifying focus for this school improvement work it was decided that the school should work towards achieving the national Standard for quality management, training and development called 'Investors in People' which had a set of externally validated benchmark assessment indicators. (These have been reproduced in the Appendix to this book.)

How the 'Investors' development plan originated

The 'Investors' development plan format particularly appealed to the SMT through its clarity and goodness-of-fit with the existing School Development Plan format. The process was a similar one in several ways. In the School Development Plan the school had endeavoured to be clear about its mission, aims and objectives, and rigorous in the analysis of the current situation, and to be forward-looking and practical in the statement of plans for the future. Both the IiP development plan and the School Development Plan shared the same processes of looking at 'where we are' and at 'where we want to go next'. The key difference between the two processes was that IiP provided a check-list of sharp-edged assessment indicators for identifying shortfalls in human resource management (HRM) practice. The IiP development plan was derived from an empirical evidence base using document analysis, analysis of HRM processes, staff questionnaires and interviews.

Getting evidence for the 'Investors' plan

It was necessary first to carry out a culture audit of the school's 'culture-in-use' (Egan 1994, p39) against the 'Investors In People' benchmark indicators. The following section summarises the findings of this audit.

Document analysis

1. Analysis of the *School Development Plan* and the *five year plan* showed that there was not an explicit commitment to develop *all* staff. The plans did not address the broad development needs of all categories of staff nor were they communicated to all staff; line management accountabilities for support staff were opaque; roles of all staff lacked clarity and specificity, and target-setting was restricted primarily to senior managers. Thus the School Development Plan needed extending and improving. (IiP indicators 1.1, 1.2, 1.4, 4.3 and 4.5 were not being met – see Appendix.)

2. Analysis of the existing *staff development policy* showed that it did not apply to all staff in the school. There was no review procedure to cover all aspects of the school; line management responsibilities for training and staff development needed clarification and there was no structure available to identify explicitly the desired outcomes of training and development. There was no mention in the policy underlining the responsibility of an individual for his or her own development.

3. Analysis of the existing *staff induction policy* showed that it did not extend to all staff and was insufficiently developed to meet the national Standard. (IiP indicators 1.1, 1.4, 2.1, 2.2, 2.4, 2.5, 2.6, 3.1, 3.2, 3.3, 3.4, 4.2 and 4.5 were not being met.)

4. HRM resources identified and subsequently used for the development of all staff were not explicitly identified in the *school budget*. The HRM planning for the school did not include any statement of performance. (IiP indicators 2.1, 4.4 and 4.5 were not being met.)

5. The HRM policy was insufficiently linked to the school's *five year plan* and a*nnual operational plan.* (IiP indicators 2.2, 4.1, 4.2 and 4.4 were not being met.)

6. The school did not have a system for *communicating to all staff* the school's staff management structure nor all staff's role in supporting the achievement of the school's objectives. (IiP indicators 2.2 and 4.1 were not being met.)

7. The school *mission statement* was not circulated to all staff nor was it presented in a linguistic style which was readily accessible to all staff. (IiP indicators 1.1, 1.2 and 1.5 were not being met.)

8. The link between *capability development and performance* was not made explicit nor was it aligned with the School Development Plan. (IiP indicators 1.1, 1.2, 2.4 and 2.5 were not being met.)

Analysis of HRM processes

1. It was apparent from interviews with staff that they did not know the *major targets* in the school development plan nor were they aware of how their individual roles contributed to achieving the school's objectives. (IiP indicators 1.2, 1.3, 1.4, 1.5 and 1.6 were not being met.)

2. The school did not have a process for gauging staff satisfaction with their individual review of *training and development needs*, nor with understanding how staff felt about the efficacy of induction, training and capability development. (IiP indicators 1.1, 1.2, 1.6, 2.3, 2.4, 2.5, 2.6, 3.1, 3.2, 3.4, 3.6, 4.3 and 4.5 were not being met.)

3. The *appraisal process* did not extend to all categories of staff. It did not systematically review performance against previous work objectives, nor did it review an individual's development against a previous period's development needs, nor agree work objectives for the next planning period. These particular elements of the appraisal process were crucial to achieving the national Standard. (IiP indicators 1.1, 1.5, 2.4, 2.5, 2.6, 2.7, 3.2, 3.3, 3.4, 3.5, 3.6, 4.2, 4.3, 4.4 and 4.5 were not being met.)

4. Staff development was not linked with possible *external accreditation* (IiP indicators 2.7 and 4.2 were not being met) and *training and development records* were not kept for all staff and lacked detail. (IiP indicators 3.2, 3.5 and 4.2 were not being met.)

5. There was no *annual review* of the school's performance against the School Development Plan with specific reference to staff development and the outcomes of planned training and development interventions. (IiP indicators 4.1, 4.3 and 4.4 were not being met.)

The shortfalls identified in the 1993 audit could not be remedied immediately and so were added to the targets in the school's overall institutional Development Plan. Senior staff agreed to assume responsibility for effecting the necessary improvements. The use of force-field analysis helped to identify barriers to change in the school.

Barriers to developing HRM practice

The factors which were found to promote and impede progress in the school's HRM improvement work were located on a force-field (see Figure 10.1).

'INVESTORS' AND HRM DEVELOPMENT

FOR CHANGE	AGAINST CHANGE
● SMT and IiP Task Group	● Attitudes of some staff
● Governors	● Initiative overload
● Post-ERA demands	● Loosely-coupled organisational culture
● Need to position school	● Demands for autonomy
● Need for corporate culture	● Suspicion of unidirectional aims
● Need for improved quality management and performance management	● Antipathy to managerialism and notions of corporate rationality
● Need for asset management	● Developmental definition of appraisal
● TEC funding to support HRM	● Precedent and opposition to evaluation
● National Training Targets	● Individualised INSET model
● IiP is consonant with good management practice, appraisal and OFSTED	● Precedent and antipathy to institutionally-driven model

Figure 10.1 Force-field acting on developing HRM practice in the school

Implications

The analysis identified key individuals whose commitment was needed; defined the critical mass required to ensure the effective implementation of the changes to meet the Standard; and located the present level of commitment to the HRM changes. The detailed analysis of stakeholders' perceptions subsequently revealed that there was much work to be done by the SMT in order to gain commitment to the 'Investors' initiative, especially from key opinion leaders amongst Heads of Department and leading staff in large departments, and from some of the technicians, caretakers and cleaning staff who felt threatened by the introduction of appraisal.

Forces against change

The two questionnaires of staff perceptions provided evidence to show that several opinion leaders in major departments were opposed to the innovation. Within departments the main reasons given for their resistance to change were:

- A different assessment of the situation as to whether the change was really needed and concerns about possible deleterious effects.
- Fear of being required to change too quickly.
- Concern over initiative overload and a concomitant loss of quality in teaching and learning.

Some of the support staff were concerned about the initiative because they were fearful for their jobs, others were worried about it because it implied change and they disliked change. Within the support staff the main concern was fear of not being able to develop the new skills that would be required by the initiative. The evaluation showed that several departments disdained the idea of a corporate culture and argued that departments had little in common and were only very loosely federated in the school.

Analysis

The chief reasons given by those opposed to working toward the 'Investors' national Standard were initiative overload, they did not value the initiative or doubted its integrity or efficacy, and a few worries about appraisal (support staff). A commitment plan was developed over 18 months in order to get the necessary commitment from the critical mass of staff. Central to this plan to get more staff 'on board' was a series of workshops led by the IiP team and TEC consultants to demonstrate the benefits of working toward the Standard in terms of job satisfaction and new skills. From the staff surveys it appeared that the school had to return to the core functions of HRM suggested by Riches and Morgan (1989) namely:

(a) Influencing others and building trust.
(b) Sharing the vision and developing commitment.
(c) Developing competence and improving performance.

The 18 month commitment plan had the following strands.

At the level of organisational culture

- Influencing key middle managers and opinion leaders among the main 'blocker' departments who were identified in the staff surveys as being opposed to the initiative.
- Assuaging their fears and reassuring them that IiP would improve practice.
- Working with the support staff in a systematic and deliberate manner to promulgate the school's vision and to get a better understanding and acceptance of that vision.
- More training in departments to secure commitment to the school's vision and objectives. Here training days and seminars led by consultants and senior staff were used throughout the plan.
- Greater involvement of the governing body to share the vision.

At the level of structure

- New organisational structures needed in order to clarify line management.
- New system of performance review/appraisal for all.
- New standardised job descriptions for all staff with targets and accountabilities.
- New system of corporate induction for all new staff and not simply for the professional teaching staff.

At the level of process

- New decentralised system of identifying training needs in departments in relation to the school's objectives, and an end to the equity principle of individually negotiated 'bespoke' INSET for all – the entitlement of all staff to three INSET days irrespective of the fit with school plan targets. (The document analysis revealed the need to change the school's INSET/Training and Development policy.)
- Use of the 'tight-loose' model of accountability in departments. A 'tight-loose' system is one which uses some 'tight' centralisation and control together with 'loose' decentralisation to give local discretion and scope for initiative. Here firm control is combined with a measure of autonomy.
- Use of 'gap analysis' recommendations to improve HRM processes in respect of communications and further surveys of staff opinion in order to gauge progress.

Reflections on 'Investors in People'

The final section of the chapter reflects first on some of the costs and benefits experienced at the school of working towards the national Standard, and provides an interim evaluation of the IiP school improvement work carried out over the last two years.

Costs of proceeding

These can be summarised as follows:

- Senior management time needed to drive the initiative.
- The difficulty of maintaining the enthusiasm and tempo over the developmental period.
- The considerable financial investment needed to effect the changes.
- The cost of consultants (£550 per day).
- Organisational disruption of mock assessments.
- TEC assessment fees (£2,500 to £3,000 for IiP assessment).
- The time required to prepare and revise the portfolio of evidence.

Practical benefits of the process for school improvement

- A way to know how staff feel and think about the school's aims, objectives and direction derived from an empirical base.
- A way to raise awareness of how managers at all levels must add value to the work of others in their work teams and to improve skill levels.
- A sharp-edged method to conduct a culture audit of the school's overall HRM position in relation to the Standard to set a focused whole-school improvement agenda.
- The 'gap analysis' technique against the 24 assessment indicators is useful for managers to scrutinise training and capability development processes.
- The disinterested report from a 'critical friend' (an HRM management consultant) on the school's management provides a helpful critique of current practice.
- The whole process is a prompt to review ossified structures and policies and to challenge institutional 'mind sets' at all levels in the school.
- IiP provides a corrective to training and development predicated on individual preference, to an emphasis on tactical and strategic training and development priorities in relation to the school's Business Plan.
- There is a deliberate and systematic emphasis on training and development as a generator of added-value.
- There is a focus on evaluation of training effectiveness at all levels.
- The framework implies a continuing commitment to staff development.
- The benchmarks will help firm up sharper accountability for achievement.
- The national Standard is reassessed every three years.

Conclusion

In conclusion, the evidence from this secondary school's experience suggests that the 'Investors' initiative can provide a useful focus to help move a school from an outdated 'culture-in-use' to a 'preferred culture' (Egan 1994, p39) which best serves the long-term interests of the school. An important benefit that has emerged from this work is that 'Investors' can also provide a tangible management framework to spell out and communicate to all the constituent parts of the 'preferred culture', and that all employees may then be socialised into that 'preferred culture'.

An important point for schools to consider before starting is whether this work ought to be presented as simply 'working toward the national Standard' in the school, or as part of a more general programme for improving standards of management

Some critiques of 'Investors in People' suggest that the problem with 'off-the-shelf' culture audits from the business environment is that they encapsulate business priorities and realities, and do not fit easily with the culture of not-for-profit service organisations like schools.

This is true in some respects. In the light of some of the findings from this school's experience it is perhaps tempting to draw the conclusion that the critique is justified, and that 'Investors in People' has proved ineffective in resolving, for example, the thorny evaluation/developmental issue at the heart of the school's staff appraisal system, or the continued preference of some teachers for a personal entitlement model of training, but this is too glib. Undoubtedly, custom and practice is a bulwark to change here.

What the work has highlighted at this school is the need for the school management to clarify professional development (i.e. the long-term process of enhancement of the practitioner's classroom performance) and career development on the one hand, and the management of staff development (the enhancement of the practitioner's role as a member of staff within the school) linked to overall school development on the other (Holly and Southworth's useful distinction, 1988, p14). The evidence from the last two years suggests that 'Investors' does transfer to schools and can be harnessed to link the 'preferred culture' to staff performance, though managing the culture change may well take time because of the deep-seated norms and patterns of behaviour and values of the 'culture-in-use' in schools.

A critique of 'Investors' is that it is a wholly decontextualised and unrealistic counsel of perfection against which organisations are asked to measure their performance (Egan 1994). Again the evidence from this school's experience is that 'Investors in People' has potential to be a key element in quality management systems in schools.

142

For some teachers in the school IiP is just another business fad with more than a whiff of snake-oil. For these teachers 'Investors' does not have a legitimate place in schools because it denies their perception of teacher professionalism and is also an initiative which is not targeted directly at improving teaching and learning for the children. For other staff in the school it has certainly proved to be a tonic, especially for the non-teaching staff who report feeling part of the team now because they know more about what is going on. Whether it can be a tonic for all the troops is doubtful. For school managers, however, the implications seem to be that IiP can be a culture-change tool to help them to manage explicitly the culture of a school. It can provide an explicit framework for identifying and auditing culture-management skills and competences at all levels.

What the experience of the past two years suggests is that 'Investors in People' can be used within a school's overall HRM strategy routinely to monitor and fine-tune the school's culture just as the school would monitor and fine-tune any key asset. In this way the school may use the 'Investors' approach to strive continually to make its 'culture-in-use' congruent with its espoused culture. As an approach to the leverage of culture change in secondary schools, therefore, it does seem to provide a possible (albeit expensive) basis for continuous organisational improvement.

Note Since this chapter was written the school has been formally recognised as an 'Investor in People' (editors).

CHAPTER ELEVEN

Effective Governing Bodies, Effective Schools?

by Martin Corrick

The governing bodies of all state schools, whether maintained by direct government grant or by a local authority, have considerable responsibility in law for the activities of their schools. Is it therefore to their governors that we should turn when seeking ways to improve the effectiveness of schools? Indeed, is the present system of 'amateur', part-time governing bodies an effective way to govern schools?

To discover whether school governors are doing their job effectively we must first be certain about its nature. The function of governors is self-evidently 'to govern', but the spectrum of meanings of that verb is very large: it begins with autocracy and progresses through notions of direction and control towards a consensual politics of the modern kind – guidance, monitoring, overseeing, being responsible. Where do school governors lie on this spectrum? In *The Control of Education* Tomlinson declared that the 1986 Education Act proved that the school governing body had become 'a crucial part of the government of education'. Its powers and functions were now so great that it could be described as one of the 'new magistracies' created in the 1980s (Tomlinson 1993). Although these 'new magistrates' undoubtedly have, in theory and in law, substantial powers and duties, their exact nature is still a matter for debate. Arguably, the powers of governing bodies actually lie towards the weaker end of the spectrum. It is worth noting that their activity is usually called neither *governing* nor *government* but *governance*, a quaint and otherwise almost obsolete term which is a good deal less authoritative than either of the alternatives.

Effective governance depends not only on the meanings of both terms but on the nature of the relationship between governing bodies and schools, something that is again highly problematic. For example, it is clearly possible that a school can be effective despite an ineffective governing body; is it similarly possible that a school may be *ineffective* despite an effective governing body? Or should we define an effective governing body simply as one which ensures (encourages, allows...?) its school to be effective?

Progress in this enquiry requires a number of reasonable assumptions to be made. The first is that *effective schools* exist, and that a degree of agreement is possible on their principal characteristics. Extensive work such as the study of 57 schools conducted for the School Management Task Force (Bolam et al. 1993) has identified comprehensive sets of such characteristics. They have been communicated to schools and governors in a number of ways; for example in *Governing Bodies and Effective Schools* (DFE 1995b), a booklet distributed by the (then) Department for Education to all schools. Here, some of the principal characteristics of effective schools are identified as professional leadership, shared vision and goals, a learning environment, a concentration on teaching and learning and explicit high expectations. Creese usefully points out that such characteristics may be divided into those of a pedagogical kind (e.g. classroom practice, record-keeping), those connected with management (e.g. organisational structures, delegation), and those rather more elusive items that may be grouped under the heading of 'school ethos' (Creese 1994).

Assessing the effectiveness of governors

A taxonomy of effectiveness such as this begins to indicate areas in which the actions of governors may be significant; in which, in other words, there are opportunities for governors to be effective. For example, it appears inherently more likely that governors can influence the strategy of a school rather than make a direct impact on details of professional practice. Indeed, according to the law the work of the governing body should focus on just such areas – on 'high level' management issues such as ethos and policy. School ethos is clearly specified in both *School Governors: A Guide to the Law* (DFE 1994a) and the *Handbook for Inspection of Schools* (OFSTED 1993) as a major responsibility of the governing body. In the *Guide to the Law* the first item on a list of 'Powers and Duties of the Governing Body' is 'helping to establish (with the head) the aims and policies of the school, and how the standards of education can be improved'. Despite the somewhat clumsy phrasing it is clear enough that co-operation with the head and school improvement are intended to be central to the work of the governing body. Similarly, but with greater brevity and boldness, *Governing Bodies and Effective Schools* (DFE 1995b op. cit.) defines the three main roles of the governing body as 'To provide a strategic view', 'To act as critical friend', and

'To ensure accountability'. The term 'strategic view' assists in separating the work of governors from school management. 'Critical friend' is gaining increased currency in descriptions of the work of governors because it combines close and companionable support with a measured degree of discrimination and wider awareness. It is worth noting that the cautious phrase 'To ensure accountability' is used instead of a more definitive statement (e.g. 'to be accountable'), again indicating ambiguities inherent in the governors' role. However, in the same publication 'accountability' is further defined as a responsibility for 'good quality education', requiring that the governing body must 'answer for its actions to parents and the wider local community for its school's overall performance.'

Here, then, is a basis for a definition of the principal duties of governing bodies. We may define it with a set of six keywords: ethos, strategy, monitoring, school improvement, co-operation and accountability. This is evidently the area in which governing bodies should be working, and it is therefore the area in which we may legitimately attempt a judgement of their effectiveness.

There is, as yet, no research which specifically attempts to assess the extent to which the behaviour of governing bodies is consistent with such a definition of their role. However, there is a considerable body of research which seeks to identify the principal characteristics of governors and to describe their attitudes and some of their behaviour. An exploration of this research should begin to indicate whether governing bodies do in fact define their task in such terms, whether such notions are the currency of their discussions, whether they are in any real sense the parameters against which they assess their own work. This last point suggests another obvious characteristic that appears essential to all conceivable definitions of effectiveness: it is that governing bodies should *actively want to be effective*.

Let us at once admit that this role definition demands a high level of skill, knowledge and confidence. Strategic thinking requires a degree of detachment from immediate concerns, and at least a good working knowledge of the kinds of options and outcomes that exist at that level. It requires governors deliberately to lift their eyes from matters that may be very immediate, very pressing, very particular, and to take the long view: to think of their school not simply as a friendly institution which should be supported, but as a key element in an important state service. This role definition suggests that an effective governing body should be concerned above all to know whether their school is effective, yet capable of maintaining a relationship of trust and warmth. These are extremely demanding requirements; it would be surprising if most governing bodies were very good at them; but it remains the case that this is what governors are required to attempt.

Some initial comfort may be gained from the knowledge that governors are not by any means a 'random group of ordinary people.' In the NFER study *School Governing Bodies: Making Progress?* (Earley 1994) about 70 per cent of a large sample of chairs and governors had GCSE O level or equivalent; 44 per cent of governors and 49 per cent of chairs were graduates; 33 per cent of chairs had a professional institute final qualification; 25 per cent of governors and chairs held a teacher's certificate. It appears that these figures have remained fairly constant in recent years; a previous NFER study (Keys and Fernandes 1990) reported comparable percentages, which remained similar even when the teacher governors (almost certainly graduates) were removed from the sample. Governors are, in comparison with the population at large, extremely well educated. The task may be difficult, but these particular people have at least a running start.

Governors' views

Does their own view of their task relate to the strategic role defined by the keywords? One study (Baginsky, Baker and Cleave 1991) found that governors' perception of their role included a comparison with the board of directors of a commercial company, and that a governor was likely to think of himself or herself as a support, a consultant or a helper. Some saw themselves as watchdogs, backstops or sharers. A few saw themselves as a link, a guardian or (in a single case) a rubber stamp. While it cannot be said that these terms approach very closely the keywords above, the governors interviewed felt that the role was evolving and would continue to do so. They admitted it had a long way to go. One governor is quoted as saying:

> The educational establishment generally opposes change so it is difficult to compete. The role now is that you sit there and nod along with what has already been decided or you open up the debate without much hope of getting very far. I believe that governors are not yet having much effect – they are starting but it is still very limited. But it will change with time. (Baginsky, Baker and Cleave 1991)

This study, and others, demonstrates the danger of inferring too much about the behaviour of governors from their expressed attitudes and opinions. Baginsky and her colleagues indicate that although governors said relationships within governing bodies were generally 'happy' and 'harmonious', such observation of meetings as they were able to carry out suggested a more complex picture. In two of the schools said to have happy and harmonious relationships the meetings of the governing body were completely dominated by the head teachers and chairs, with 'little or no input from a substantial proportion of the governing body'. However, the study goes on to note that 'The atmosphere in both cases was cordial and the governors appeared to be quite content with the state of affairs'. Forty-four governors were asked how confident they felt about contributing to the various areas which governors deliberate upon. Twenty-eight said they were 'very confident' about the curriculum, a figure which appears very high, particularly when placed beside the admission of some governors that they 'had not questioned assumptions or definitions with which they felt some unease because this might have been interpreted as questioning teachers' professionalism.' There is evidently a tendency for governors to define their performance at a higher level than can be confirmed by objective evidence.

About half the case study schools said that a draft of the school aims written by the head teacher had gone through without discussion. The head teachers 'acknowledged the theoretical power and responsibilities of governors but failed to see how they could be implemented'. They said that 'few governors spoke with any certainty' on questions of governance and management. In their conclusion the authors state:

> Many governors in this study were reluctant to challenge professionals on educational issues and yet believed it essential for the curriculum to be at the centre of all their deliberations. On the rare occasions when comments or queries appeared to question aspects of the curriculum in the school, head-teachers and sometimes the teacher governors tended to become defensive and found it difficult to deal with the situation .... In the schools in this study only two headteachers [out of nine] believed the governors took an active role in decision-making. (Baginsky, Baker and Cleave 1991, p115)

Other studies in the early 1990s confirm this view. The conclusions of a study of 25 schools in the north of England by Sheffield University Management School were that the transition to Local Management of Schools (LMS) had resulted in a stronger role for head teachers rather than governors:

> Despite the greater responsibilities now resting with boards of governors, the headteacher is now in an even stronger and more demanding position than before LMS. The head is the chief policy maker of the school, and the chief executive ... all too often, governing bodies are, whilst perhaps willing, unprepared for their role. (Shearn et al. 1992)

The most recent, comprehensive and authoritative study of governing bodies is that undertaken by Earley (1994). One chapter of his report is concerned with the results of an open-ended enquiry in which the sample of head teachers, chairs and governors were asked to give their views on the main features of an effective governing body. These are listed according to the frequency with which they were mentioned. The heads most frequently said that the most important feature was that the governing body gave time and was committed to the school. The chairs broadly agreed, but gave equal importance to sharing and teamwork. Rank-and-file governors were somewhat more deferential; their most frequently mentioned characteristic was 'working well with head and staff'. It is possible to detect areas of agreement among these responses: greatest emphasis was placed on sharing, support and involvement, with some-what less emphasis on skill and knowledge. A few responses fell outside these two main groups and were mentioned relatively infrequently; these included the idea of the critical friend, an awareness of governors' roles and responsibilities and a clear view of the school's aims. The latter was, on average, the least frequently mentioned feature of all.

I have elsewhere considered (Corrick 1995) some of the implications of this extremely revealing study, but some points require repetition. We should note that the features that governors considered most desirable in an effective governing body are remarkable principally for their *passivity*. This evidence clearly suggests that governing bodies are primarily concerned with accommodating themselves to their schools, rather than applying their collective powers to the direction of the school. Co-operation has the highest priority. Involvement with key functions such as policy making, monitoring, or acting as a critical friend are the eighth and ninth features of a list which does not refer to school ethos, strategy, improvement, accountability or effectiveness at all. Fifteen features are mentioned on the list; only two or perhaps three are conceivably related to a *dynamic* definition of the governors' role.

A contrasting list of factors that these governors considered likely to hinder their effectiveness is completely dominated by 'lack of time'. Yet the governors (excluding chairs) surveyed by Earley claimed, on aver-age, to spend no more than eight hours per term preparing for meetings, a figure not dissimilar to the ten to twelve hours recorded by Keys and Fernandes in 1991. It is difficult to be convinced that this is an impossibly large time commitment, sufficient to create significant pressure on time. I would therefore argue that this attitude is essentially a symptom of inse-curity in the role rather than a real difficulty. Governors undoubtedly perceive the role as a serious undertaking, but many, perhaps most, are unsure both of its exact nature and of their own ability to perform it; this insecurity generates a high level of anxiety expressed in terms of 'so much to do, so little time'.

Earley also includes a list of the main topics discussed at length by his sample of governing bodies during 1992–93, placed in order of the fre-quency with which they were mentioned. First place is taken by resources, followed by building maintenance, annual parents' meetings, staff appointments, the school development plan, curriculum issues, staffing structure, aims and objectives of the school and various other topics. Once again there is little correlation with keywords relating to the principal duties of governors. Routine and relatively minor matters are evidently allowed to take precedence over discussions of ethos, strategy, monitoring, school improvement or effectiveness.

It appears that governors are usually reluctant to consider areas other than those in which they feel they may have some relevant knowledge and experience, and in which they do not see themselves as intruding upon the preserve of the professional staff. Governors do not, on this evidence, display an awareness of recent debates on education. They appear entirely to lack an overview or context in which their particular school may be placed. There is no reference to the quality of teaching and learning. There is evidently very little consciousness of national findings such as those of OFSTED and the Audit Commission, indicating areas in which some schools are still failing to reach a satisfactory standard. And it is worth noting at this stage how closely the topics discussed by governors, apart from aims and objectives of the school, can be identified with management rather than governance.

Heads or governors: who's in charge?

The respondents to the enquiry of Bolam et al. (1993) were teachers and head teachers of schools that considered themselves to be effectively managed, and the picture given here of governors is considerably more pessimistic even than that already described. The report declares that 'only limited progress has been made toward increasing the influence of governors on school policy and practice', and 'school governors seem to defer to the headteacher as the lead professional on the majority of issues'. It is firmly dismissive of the notion that governing bodies are yet anywhere near a reasonable level of effectiveness: 'Asked about the nature and extent of the contribution made by governors to school policy, respondents repeatedly indicated that this was very limited ...'. Governors 'focused more on 'bricks and mortar' issues ... than ... curriculum matters.' There were 'repeated references to governors being seen to rubber stamp conclusions and decisions reached by headteachers ... '. The report concludes by saying:

> Although relationships between governors and staff in most of the sample of schools appeared to be positive, serious doubts were expressed in the schools visited, by governors as well as staff, about the effectiveness of the governors in contributing to the management of the schools ...

And:

The findings relating to the roles and effectiveness of governors in school management are disquieting but are consistent with other, impressionistic evidence. They suggest the need for a detailed and specific review of policy and practice in this area. (Bolam et al. 1993, p125 and p131)

The general tenor of this report is that the central and vital role in the direction of a school belongs not to the governing body but to the head teacher. It is hardly surprising, therefore, that the study finds that a feature of effective schools is that 'Governors are ready to follow the headteacher's advice on most issues; staff and governors have a positive relationship.' (By this measure, we may note, a completely moribund governing body might be considered effective.) The head's vision for the school is said to be a crucial factor. Those heads best able to articulate such a vision 'gave every indication of having debated at length educational issues and values, of having engaged critically with the relevant literature, and of having worked out for themselves a basic philosophy of education to which they subscribed ... '. According to this report (which we might define as 'professionally inclined') it is the head, not the governing body, of an effective school who must display a consciousness of the keywords of effectiveness.

Further evidence for a continuing lack of effectiveness of most governing bodies could be adduced, but I doubt whether it would add greatly to the picture already established. One of the most elegant and careful summaries of the current position is that contained in paragraph 6 of the Commentary to the *1993-4 Annual Report* of Her Majesty's Chief Inspector of Schools:

Evidence from this year's report suggests that governing bodies are, on occasion and for a variety of reasons, deflected from discharging fully their key function of strategic direction. In plain language this means asking relatively simple questions: about standards of pupils' achievement; about behaviour and attendance; about homework, attitudes and expectations. Where such questions are asked, and answers sought, governing bodies are offering schools the informed support of the critical friend. Where they are not asked, governors will have only a limited impact on standards and quality. Conversely, some governors take too close an interest in the day-to-day work of schools. To become too involved in this way is to run the risk of undermining the management and leadership of the headteacher. (OFSTED 1995d)

Contributing factors

I have already suggested that one of the reasons for the evident lack of effectiveness among governing bodies is hostility among teachers and head teachers to their increased powers. This resistance to the involvement of 'outsiders' is also demonstrated by academics and senior educationists throughout the service, and hence the discussion of school effectiveness tends neither to involve governors nor to consider their role in achieving it. For example Sayer, in *The Future Governance of Schools* makes only a handful of passing references to governors, usually in the context of community links (Sayer 1993). He does not for a moment consider that governing bodies should in future carry the major responsibility for schools; instead, he envisages a fully professional service managed by professionals who at some time in the future will have confirmed their professionalism through membership of a body such as the emergent General Teaching Council (of which he was, at the time of writing, the secretary). It is the professional teacher, not the parent, the politician, the community, or (least of all) the professional manager that Sayer, with many other educationists, argues should properly be in charge of schools.

If most head teachers are uneasy about the powers of governors, experience suggests that many classroom teachers feel actually threatened by them. Indeed, they often appear unduly susceptible to such anxieties, probably because teaching does not offer the social status, self-esteem, emotional security and strong value structure of other professions. Bearing in mind the pressured nature of teaching as an occupation, and the denigration that teachers have suffered from government and others in recent years, it is possible to feel considerable sympathy for them. The irony, of course, is that their fears are mostly groundless; governing bodies usually do what head teachers tell them to do. However, an awareness of the anxieties of teachers undoubtedly inhibits governors who themselves lack a clear and uncompromised view of their role and their authority.

Education professionals commonly pay lip service to the role of governors but offer little real recognition. For example, although the OFSTED *Framework* published in the *Handbook for the Inspection of Schools* makes a number of references to governors' responsibilities for strategic planning and monitoring, in practice OFSTED inspectors appear to take a different view. In a study of 67 OFSTED reports collected between 1992 and 1994, Creese (1994) finds an essentially low and irregular level of reference to governors. There was little evidence that inspectors placed the work of governors very centrally; for example, they visited few governors' meetings. References to the 'key issues for action' rarely invoked governors: only six of the reports contained a specific reference to the need for action on key issues by the governing body. Although a range of comments about governors was found in the body of the reports, particularly under headings such as 'Efficiency of the School' and 'Management and Administration', these had little consistency or importance.

Assembling his gleanings from the reports, Creese lists the kinds of expectations that some inspectors evidently have of governing bodies. They should:

- work closely with the head and staff;
- fulfil their legal responsibilities, particularly for school policies;
- be involved in setting the aims of the school;
- be involved in school improvement through the school development plan;
- ensure that resources are managed efficiently and effectively by monitoring the outcomes of decisions.

This is a low key, passive model closely related to the co-operative and management-centred paradigm that we have already noted. It is interesting to observe the cautious phrase 'be involved in', suggesting that the OFSTED inspectors, identifying with the professional view, cannot bring themselves to say that governing bodies should *determine* the aims of the school.

Creese considers that the evidence of these OFSTED reports is not conclusive; the work of governing bodies may not be mentioned simply because it is considered satisfactory. In the light of other evidence this looks doubtful; it is surely the case that inspectors simply do not consider governors to be a particularly significant factor in the effectiveness of schools.

Governor training

The evident lack of effectiveness among governors may also be related to the kind of training they receive. It is arguable that, instead of seeking to empower governors by giving them access to, and familiarity with, high level strategic ideas, the governor training curriculum has been allowed to accumulate an indiscriminate mass of highly detailed material mostly concerned with school management. Consider this list of the topics included in training (as reported by Earley 1994) which is in my experience quite typical:

Roles and functions of school governors	Local Management of Schools
Recruitment and selection	Personnel management
Effective meetings	Chairing meetings
School visits	Annual Reports
Annual parents' meetings	School development planning
The National Curriculum	Special educational needs
Equal opportunities	Multicultural education

Sex education	Collective worship and RE
Preparing for inspection	GM status
School and community links	Dealing with parents
Behaviour	Discipline and exclusion
Health and safety	Premises
Teacher appraisal	

This enormous training programme is designed, we should not forget, for part-time volunteers who spend rather less than an hour a week about their business. Such a curriculum suggests the lack of a clear overview by the LEAs who design and deliver the majority of training, an amazing lack of awareness of the impossibility of providing so large a curriculum to a continuously changing audience of 350,000 people with any degree of effectiveness. It suggests a view of education that is completely dominated by detailed professional concerns; indeed, it may even suggest an underlying desire to ensure that governors drown in the complexity of education and hence are incapable of significant action. It may suggest that LEAs may see governor training as a convenient way of maintaining their own grasp on an education service that has been forcibly distanced from them by government. Nor is this all that the LEAs do; under the heading of 'governor support' most of them submit governors to a considerable torrent of paper – information, regulations, policies, recommendations, advice, updates – which may indeed further contribute to governors' feelings that they have insufficient time to do their job properly.

It is clearly arguable that this kind of training curriculum drives governors not towards their proper role but towards interference in the management of schools. Symptomatic of this is a recent evaluation report on the governor training service of a large LEA; its main findings cited 'Three areas in which governors need further help or clarification: the relationship between planned savings and building projects; the facilities of the computerised financial management system (FMS); the management of instrumental music' (Edwards et al. 1994). These are very clearly management issues, and have little to do with strategic planning; yet these inspectors thought governors needed to be told about them.

How secure are governors in their role?

A third reason for the relative ineffectiveness of governing bodies is the insecurity of governors themselves. One of the most remarkable findings of the latest NFER study is that a third of the governors consulted, and no fewer than half the chairs, thought governing bodies have too much responsibility (Earley 1994). And that view was shared by 60 per cent of heads. Given these fundamental doubts about the correctness of their role, it is hardly possible to envisage school governors taking on anything like the role defined by the keywords. The evidence is that governors feel both humble and hard-pressed; they feel doubtful about their role and about their knowledge of what they see as a highly complex and professional business; as a result they are essentially characterised not by a desire to be effective but by *deference*: they feel that their principal duty is to adapt to the school, rather than the school respond to them.

On reflection, this finding should not be surprising. Although the law gives them responsibility, governors acquire their status, role and significance from the school itself; they begin, and continue, in a position of dependency. The school is the dominant entity. Governors come, governors go, the school remains. The great majority of their information comes from the school. Its staff is trained, qualified, experienced, full-time and paid. In comparison, governors may appear, both to themselves and to teachers, as untrained, unqualified, inexperienced, part-time and unpaid. They may be perceived as bumbling amateurs, perhaps even as voyeurs, a nuisance, an actual hindrance to the proper functioning of the school.

Crucially, few governors appear to have had opportunities to think about education in any deliberate, coherent and speculative way – for example, to consider the purposes of schools, standards, styles of teaching, variations upon the curriculum or choices for future development. Even though a considerable number of school governors are teachers or are employed in education, it is not evident that this enables them to operate at a strategic level; indeed, the reverse may be true. It is clear enough that, far too often, minor matters and a dense mass of routine business are permitted to dominate meetings and drive out discussion of strategic issues. On occasion, proper discussion is obstructed by head teachers or local authority officers determined to maintain their own agendas. Anecdotal evidence suggests that, among their peers, head teachers sound like Victorian wives: the best governing bodies are those who trouble them least. Heads are given immense power by their almost complete control of information, and the dense forest of jargon and regulation surrounding education is easily portrayed as the (unfortunate) reason why change cannot occur.

In these circumstances it is not surprising that it is difficult for governors to question the management of a school and the actions of its staff, or to feel confident in defining school policies. Governors do not want to upset anyone; indeed, the evidence suggests that they wish at all costs to avoid doing so. Being a governor in England or Wales is a traditional thing, one of those decent, respectable but not tremendously significant things that one does, like being a parish councillor or on the committee of the community association. It is not expected that governors will achieve significant change. The self-image of governors is in most cases worthy, deferential and conservative; few wish to risk controversy. Quite contrary to the fears expressed by teachers, the great majority of governors simply want to do what the school wants them to do.

There is a fourth reason for the relative ineffectiveness of governing bodies, to which I have already briefly alluded. It is that the task given to school governors is extremely difficult, and may indeed be beyond what should be demanded of ordinary citizens acting in a voluntary capacity without thorough training.

Four reasons, therefore, for what is undeniably a less than effective performance by most governing bodies: the hostility of teachers and educationists; the inappropriateness of most governor training; the inherent deference of governors; and the difficulty of the task given to them.

The effectiveness of governors: does it matter?

It is hard to deny, on this evidence, that the authority given to governors is something of a sham, but neither government nor the educational establishment appears concerned. If governors are not able to accept their responsibilities, the quality of a school is almost entirely dependent on whether it happens to have an effective head. There are no checks and balances within the institution, no one other than the head with an overview, no parental or community input, no real accountability. Governors generate a great deal of work, particularly on the part of heads; this work should make a clear contribution to school effectiveness.

To resolve these problems the role of governors could be simplified, more clearly defined, and separated from management. Tyrrell Burgess indicates a promising approach when he asks how governors can be accountable 'if they do not actually do anything', and answers his own question by saying that the solution lies in their securing performance by others: 'The chief function of a governing body is to be the body to whom the professionals, the head and staff, are accountable' (Burgess 1992). A definition such as this does not require governors to become managers; it implies that it is the school's job to explain and justify itself clearly to those who stand at the interface between school and society. Further, it is possible to envisage a set of clearly definable 'central tasks' which are the specific responsibility of the governing body. In line with such ideas, a more realistic and functional definition of the governors' role could be constructed.

Secondly, the training of governors could be restructured to provide a simpler and clearer focus. Arguably, training ('education' is probably a more appropriate term) should be compulsory, and defined by a national curriculum which can be delivered to all governors. Possibly, governors should be supported and monitored not by LEAs but by an independent, specialist body, perhaps developed from an existing organisation such as Action for Governors' Information and Training (AGIT). Certainly, the principal objectives of training should be to confirm to governors their right confidently to ask the 'relatively simple questions' defined by the Chief Inspector, to provide sufficient knowledge of what those questions might be, and to assist governors to conduct a meaningful debate with their school about its current state and future development.

Governing bodies, I would argue, can have an important role in school development or school improvement, though until recently researchers and OFSTED have largely ignored it. Indeed, the recognition of a need to address this problem is just becoming evident from such publications as the DFE's *Governing Bodies and Effective Schools* (1995b) – written by school effectiveness researchers – and a joint paper by OFSTED and the Audit Commission, *Lessons in teamwork: How school governing bodies can become more effective* (1995). But there is some way to go before we are able to say with any conviction that a school's effectiveness is the result of its effective governing body or that governing bodies are key players (partners?) in the school improvement process.

CHAPTER TWELVE

School Development Planning and Strategic Planning for School Improvement

by Brian Fidler

School development planning has been introduced to schools in England and Wales as a process which can be used for improving schools from within. However, school development planning and strategic planning are not synonymous. It is perfectly possible to be practising school development planning according to the prescriptions whilst the school is failing to attract pupils and heading for closure. Strategic planning is much more fundamental than school development planning. It considers the basic position of the organisation and its future.

Origins of school development planning

Several influences came together at the end of the 1980s which led to the creation of school development planning. The 1988 Education Reform Act:

(a) delegated financial management to school level and which required a financial plan, and
(b) created a National Curriculum which schools were required to implement.

The 1986 Education Act had previously reformed the provision of In-Service Education of Teachers (INSET), requiring school needs to be considered. This required a mechanism for identifying school needs for staff development in addition to teachers identifying their own personal and professional development needs. Some LEAs, notably Enfield and ILEA, pioneered a form of School Development Plan from 1985. The Thomas Report on improving primary schools in inner London recommended that schools should have a plan which took account of the policies of the LEA, the views of parents, the needs of children and the capacities of the staff (ILEA 1985). In Enfield the process was intended to help schools through a period of change (Goddard and Leask 1992). Such plans since they identified areas for school development also implicitly if not explicitly also identified staff development needs in order to implement these plans.

These were the reasons but there was also the experience of two developments in the late 1970s and early 1980s on which to build. Responding to the 'Great Debate' in 1976 many LEAs had implemented schemes of school self-evaluation as a means of demonstrating the accountability of schools for the quality of their work. The value of such schemes was questioned (Clift 1982). There were some doubts about the accuracy of the account that was rendered but even more about the ability and motivation of schools to set about improving those aspects of their work which the self-evaluation had identified as in need of attention. The difficulties of doing so in one school in the period 1986–89 are described by Glover (1990). The second, and related development, was a project begun by the Schools Council for Curriculum and Examinations to aid schools both to evaluate their practice and plan developments. This was the GRIDS (Guidelines for Review and Internal Development in Schools) project (McMahon et al. 1984). This was intended to retain the benefit of structure from the LEA schemes but to allow teachers to choose what to review and how in the hope of engendering motivation after the review (Clift 1987).

Although there has been prior experience of whole-school working on developmental activities in many schools, in introducing school development planning there has been a lack of realisation that development planning itself is an innovation in its own right (Constable 1994). LEAs have provided varying degrees of documentation and courses to support the process.

Whilst those in education built on existing knowledge in this ad hoc way, others looked at the experience of other organisations in planning their future (Fidler 1989). Since the 1960s commercial organisations have engaged in strategic planning as a means of planning the future of the whole organisation. During the 1980s such planning was also expanding into the not-for-profit sector. The other factor introduced into education by the 1988 Act and which school development planning did not address was the funding of schools according to the number of pupils in the school. This put a premium on the competitive position of the school and its ability to recruit pupils. It is at this more fundamental level of survival that strategic planning starts.

As school development planning has progressed it has come closer to strategic planning and the time may be right for a fusing of the two processes with school development planning as the means of implementing the strategy identified by strategic planning. However, before considering strategic planning we need to understand school development planning.

School Development Planning

The Department of Education (DES) funded a short project to produce guidance for schools on planning. The results of this work were circulated as advice to schools in 1989 and 1991 (DES 1989,1991) with a book *The Empowered School* giving further guidance (Hargreaves and Hopkins, 1991). They stated:

> The purpose of development planning is to improve the quality of teaching and learning in a school through the successful management of innovation and change. (p.3)

The process was based on a cyclical model of change. With the stages representing the following four questions:

- Where is the school now?
- What changes do we need to make?
- How shall we manage these changes over time?
- How shall we know whether our management of change has been successful?

The stages are:

- *Audit*: a school reviews its strengths and weaknesses.

  An audit involves questioning current provision and practice in a systematic and self-critical way: comparing what the school is striving to achieve with what is actually happening. The audit clarifies the nature of a school's weaknesses and guides the action needed to put things right. (Hargreaves and Hopkins, 1991; p.31).

- *Construction*: priorities for development are selected and then turned into specific targets.

  A restricted number of coherent priorities are decided and approved by governors. These then have to be turned into specific action plans. A target is specified, how it will be evaluated, what is required to achieve it and who is responsible for its achievement.

- *Implementation*: the planned priorities and targets are implemented.

  Implementation involves sustaining commitment to the developments, monitoring progress and taking action on problems as they arise. Achievements need to be noted and progress information given to governors.

- *Evaluation*: the success of implementation is checked.

As targets are achieved the process needs to be reviewed and before the start of the next year the progress of the plan needs to be evaluated to inform next year's plan.

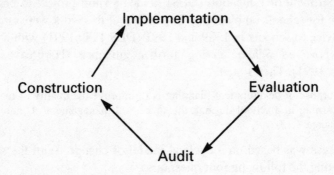

Figure 12.1 Getting Started

Interestingly the model (DES 1989; Hargreaves and Hopkins 1991) does not have a stage which considers 'where are we aiming?'. This stage only appears in the anonymously written second DES (1991) booklet. Instead the original model moves straight from the audit stage into constructing courses of action. The audit has reviewed the school's mission, aims and values, central and local policies, recent reviews, teacher appraisal targets, and the views of others. This is largely inward looking and reactive compared to the equivalent process in strategic management which is outward looking, questions the mission, aims and values and includes a vision of the future as a proactive element.

Hargreaves and Hopkins (1991) caution:

> To avoid innovation overload, the school should be firm in its resolve to prioritize, and should not attempt to develop everything at once. (p18)

There are two ideas which inform the process and the choice of priorities. The first is the importance of 'management arrangements'. These are subsequently identified (Hargreaves and Hopkins 1994) as organisational structure and organisational culture. Organisational structure represents the structuring of positions and decision-making machinery in the school (Fidler 1992) and organisational culture represents the taken-for-granted assumptions about how people work together or 'recipe' for solving organisational problems (Fidler 1989). Briefly, Hargreaves and

Hopkins believed that a collaborative mode of working was required by which teachers and head teacher all contributed and all had responsibilities for development. There would also be a new relationship with the governors and a partnership with the LEA.

The second, related to the first, is a distinction between root and branch innovations. Hargreaves and Hopkins see root innovations as more fundamental and generating the base for branch innovations. Root innovations include suitable management arrangements and a staff development policy. Once these are in place other development can build on them. For example, with these in place, developing a new assessment policy in the school will be much more straightforward.

Much of the work of schools is ongoing or maintaining the performance of current operations. Development is in tension with this maintenance function. The challenge is to combine the two.

Hargreaves and Hopkins (1991) recognise that the development planning process is more important than the actual plan itself. As Constable, Norton and Abbott (1991) discovered, understanding seems to pass through three stages:

(a) a focus on the plan as a document
(b) a recognition that the process is more important than the plan
(c) a realisation that the management of planning is the key to successful development planning.

Development planning has been reported in other countries. However, since the school context is very different in these countries and the process is critically dependent on context, such findings, unless the context is similar, are not directly relevant to the situation in England and Wales. The degree of similarity in the context is a matter which needs empirical enquiry, not an uncritical acceptance. In addition to the historical context of school self-evaluation referred to earlier, other factors which played a part in creating the context for school development planning in England and Wales are the following:

– historically great discretion for decision-making at school level
– widespread management training for head teachers and others, particularly since 1983
– management development during career progression to head teacher.

Other educational systems without these factors are not likely to have similar experiences. It is widely agreed that each school needs to start the process in its own way, depending on its history of involvement in self-evaluation and development planning.

School development planning in practice

General picture

Although there has been advice and guidance to schools on how to engage in school development planning there has been relatively little research to indicate how it works in practice. As part of a recent investigation (Mortimore et al. 1994) questionnaires were sent to all LEAs in England and Wales. It emerged that school development planning was widespread, with about 75 per cent of LEAs reporting that all or almost all schools had development plans (SDPs) in 1991–92. A quarter expected plans or priorities to be submitted to the LEA for approval. Over a half collected the plans and a third required a summary of priorities. The overwhelming majority analysed aspects of the plans. Eighty per cent referred 'often' to SDPs in their inspection and monitoring of schools but only 60 per cent as part of their support for schools.

All LEAs expected schools to include curriculum and staffing matters in their plans. Most LEAs expected teaching staff and governors to be involved in producing the plans and most involved inspectors and advisers. Only a quarter involved parents. It should be remembered that these accounts were provided by LEA officials and therefore are likely to give a view of what was expected to take place.

In detail

The more detailed experiences of development planning, whilst not directly questioning its value, do raise issues which suggest that:

(a) practice is varied;
(b) staff involvement may be less desired than proponents assume;
(c) agreement on priorities may be less consensual and more conflictual than envisaged;
(d) the rational planning cycle may not be sustainable because of unpredictable external and internal influences;
(e) external imposition of particular forms of planning may be counterproductive.

It should also be borne in mind that some of the detailed evidence comes from schools which were specifically chosen for their interest and experience in development planning (Wallace 1991a; McGilchrist, et al. 1994). Such schools could be assumed to have better developed practice than schools generally.

There is a final, more general observation on the recent pattern of reform in England and Wales. The following factors have been inimical to planning at school level:

1. Pace of externally imposed changes.
2. Lack of a comprehensive timetable to predict the timing of different external impositions.
3. Lateness of documentation to implement mandated changes.
4. The untested impracticality of a number of curriculum and assessment requirements.
5. The withdrawal of some curriculum requirements after some schools have planned their introduction.

Thus, it can be argued, although development planning was intended to help schools deal with multiple innovations, the factors above were likely to discredit any rational planning process. Any evidence on the operation of development planning in the period before the Dearing moratorium on external change announced in 1994 should therefore be considered with this in mind. This may go some way to explaining Constable's remark about:

> the well worn joke about the man at the bar with too many glasses to carry, who complains that an offered tray is one more thing to carry. This is not an uncommon reaction to school development planning. (Constable, Norton and Abbott 1991, p6)

When schools are so busy and harassed there is not time to stand back and recognise the glasses from the tray.

The most wide ranging coverage in depth of school development planning was carried out in the North East of England in 1991 (Biott, Easen and Atkins 1994). This study was based on a sample of 57 schools in nine LEAs (24 primary, 19 secondary, 8 special and 6 middle schools). Data was gathered by interviews with each school's head, a middle manager, and a main grade teacher. The following gives the percentage of plans which covered:

Curriculum (95%)
Staff development (82%)
Fabric (46%)
Community (39%)
Finance (37%)
No plan (2%)

Thus plans are highly concerned with curriculum development and the associated staff development, although there is a wider coverage in a minority of plans. The pattern was similar for both primary and secondary schools.

To compare planning processes in different schools Biott and colleagues (1994) created a set of six dimensions (for each dimension the two extreme positions are indicated):

1. Construction relationship dimension: how those involved interacted – integrated/separated

2. Managing planning dimension: extent to which SDP was integrated with management – organistic/mechanistic

3. Quality assurance dimension: extent to which success criteria were used – explicit success criteria for quality/no criteria

4. Content dimension: comprehensiveness and internal coherence – holistic/singular

5. Change dimension: extent to which used to support change or maintain existing policies and practices – development/maintenance

6. Participation and control: extent to which control exercised by head and SMT – partnership/retained power.

Each dimension has a number of different positions on the dimension and in most cases there is an order. For example, construction has the following four possibilities:

- enmeshed: all discussion face-to-face
- communicative: bilateral discussions usually on basis of expertise
- connected: individuals contributed ideas to a 'planner'
- separated: equivalent to 'co-ordination by stapler'.

The position of each school on each of the six dimensions can be plotted so that schools' practices can be compared. On each dimension there were found to be large differences between schools.

Planning process

An important finding from Biott, Easen and Atkins (1994) was that while head teachers regarded staff involvement in the planning process as desirable, staff did not always regard involvement in a similar light. As they reported:

> This questions the extent to which teachers' involvement in formal whole-school planning and democratic decision-making might be 'empowering' for them. (p85)

Similar findings were reported by Constable (1994) also from the North East of England. She found that some teachers were unaware of plans, others had been involved in a minor way or only informally. Since there appeared to have been relatively little involvement of teaching staff it was not clear how rewarding staff would have found the experience, but the inference is, that because the plan was being completed for external consumption, teachers were not particularly keen to become more involved.

An associated issue raised by researchers in one case study school (Newman and Pollard 1994) is: how is agreement reached on planning priorities? They cite the example of a new head teacher who wished to work collaboratively with staff but who also had certain changes that she wished to make. Although the picture is clouded by rather poor management, the issue of conflict is raised which is quite absent from any of the prescriptive work on development planning. In this example all the dissenters left and it is probably this aspect which is atypical rather than the lack of agreement on priorities.

As a result of recent work in nine primary schools – chosen, from 18 nominated by LEA officers on the criteria of being engaged in, and interested in, development planning and which might be interested in taking part in the research, and to give a range of sizes, locations and experience of planning – McGilchrist et al. (1994) give some preliminary findings on styles of development planning. They identify four types:

(a) *the rhetorical plan*: there was no shared ownership and the document was not a working one.
(b) *the singular plan*: this was largely produced by the head teacher and was not a working document. There was no impact on teachers or children.
(c) *the cooperative plan*: teachers played a part in producing the plan and senior staff managed the process. The plan was a working document and was linked to professional development of teachers and there was limited evidence of impact on children.
(d) *the corporate plan*: there was a united effort to improve, with teachers managing aspects of the plan and feeling responsible for outcomes. A link could be discerned between the development of the school, teachers and children.

There was no suggestion that these were stages in the development of planning. A surprising finding was that the more effective plans were more complex. Planning for improvement was embedded in the culture of the school and finance and professional development were linked to the implementation of the plan. McGilchrist et al. (1994) comment that for self-improvement by the school there needs to be well developed self-evaluation processes. Surprisingly there seems to have been little relationship between any LEA inspections and the development plan. However, data was collected before OFSTED inspections of primary schools began in September 1994. In reviewing these findings it should be remembered that although they are based on interviews and observations over two years, they cover only nine schools and these were not randomly chosen.

Wallace (1991a, 1991b, 1994) and Hutchinson (1993) cite examples where the requirements for particular forms of development planning by LEAs and sudden and arbitrary changes to those requirements have distorted and exacerbated planning problems in schools. Wallace (1994), as a result of following eight primary schools and three secondary schools for periods of six months to a year in the period 1989–92, pointed out a number of occasions on which internal (e.g. a new distribution of teaching periods, maternity leave) and external (e.g. a marketing initiative in response to another school, curriculum reforms) influences forced schools to work outside the existing development plans. In multi-racial primary schools subject to reorganisation by their LEA, in conditions which Wallace describes as turbulent, he suggest that a more flexible form of planning may be needed. In these exceptional schools this may be the case, his other examples could be covered by strategic planning

The concept of strategy

Although the words 'strategy' and 'strategic' are beginning to permeate education, the terms are used in a general way which seems to imply little more than long term and makes no contact with work on strategy which has been applied to other organisations. This section tries to clarify these complex ideas and to make them distinctive.

The distinctive features of strategy involve:

1. A consideration of the long term.
2. Planning the future of the whole school in an integrated way.
3. Taking account of future trends in the world outside the school.
4. Taking account of the school's present, and likely future, resources.

Although I shall loosely refer to 'strategic planning', there are in fact at least four distinct approaches to strategy (Whittington 1993) which make different assumptions about the aims of the organisation and the extent of the predictability of the environment. I shall describe an approach which is suitable for non-profit-making organisations which have pluralistic aims and which use strategy to plan for the future.

Strategic planning

The essence of strategy is strategic thinking. This is proactive. It tries to anticipate the future rather than waiting for it to happen and then reacting in crisis. It recognises strategic decisions which will have major implications for the organisation in the future. Strategic thinking can be solely in the minds of individuals (Steiner 1979) or it can be formally expounded by a strategic planning process. The advantages of a formal process are that:

- it is systematic with less chance of important issues being ignored, and
- it is open and communicative so that others can join in.

The following are two models which each illustrate different aspects of strategic planning. In that sense they are complementary rather than alternatives. Further details of these and other models are in Fidler et al. (1996).

Model 1 – Basic model of strategic management

This is based upon the ideas of Barry (1986) after substantial experience with small non-profit organisations in the USA. He gives the following steps:

1. Get organised.
2. Take stock.
3. Develop a strategy.
4. Draft and refine the plan.
5. Implement the plan.

Fidler et al. (1996) have adapted this to pick out three organising decisions about how to carry out the strategy process and separated these from the three substantive parts – analysis (2), choice (3) and implementation (5). This model incorporates the three phases of the process (2, 3, and 5) and deals with two important issues about how the process is conducted (1 and 4).

A diagram incorporating organising decisions and decisions on substantive content based on this model is shown (Figure 12.2). In addition to the five stages described above, a sixth has been added – making decisions about how to choose strategy. In Barry's five steps this was treated as part of developing strategy but seems more appropriately treated as the third organising decision.

○ organising decision

□ strategy process

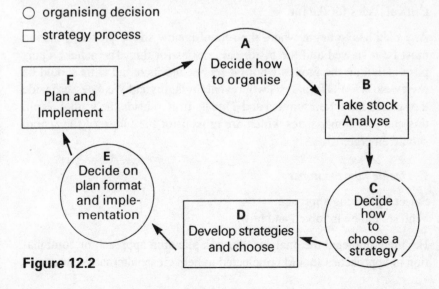

Figure 12.2

The organising decisions A, C, E and the strategy processes B, D and F are described below.

A *Decide how to organise*

Decide whether to develop a strategic plan.
Obtain commitment.
Determine if outside help is needed.
Outline a formal planning process that fits.
Form a planning team.

This is where decisions about the planning process itself are made. Having decided to engage in strategic planning, all those involved need to be convinced that this is a process worth spending time and effort on. Depending on the confidence of the school, the availability of a suitable consultant and finance to employ such help, external help may be a great advantage. A basic planning process needs to be decided that is suitable for the particular school and its staff. Questions such as the following need to be answered. Who is going to take part? From whom is evidence to be collected? Who is to be consulted? How are decisions to be made? Finally, the group who are going to carry out most of the work needs to be formed on an appropriate basis.

B *Take stock – Analyse*

History and present situation.
Mission.
Opportunities and threats.
Strengths and weaknesses.
Critical issues for the future.

Any plan has to begin where the school is now so the present situation must be reviewed and the historical reasons for this. The school's purpose including the groups whom it serves and its broad aims should be reviewed. A SWOT analysis will reveal Strengths and Weaknesses inside the school and Opportunities and Threats from outside the school. From this analysis some issues which are crucial for the future of the school should emerge.

C *Decide how to choose*

Select a planning approach.
Who should be involved and how.

Having completed the analysis phase, a planning approach or combination of approaches should be selected to help create alternative strategies for the future. The approaches are:

- developing a vision;
- identifying and resolving strategic issues (Bryson 1988);
- setting goals;
- and a cost-benefit approach.

These are described in more detail in Fidler et al. (1996). Decisions are also needed about how this should be organised. Do all operate all methods or do groups each use one method and compare results?

D *Develop strategies and choose*

Identify and evaluate alternatives.
Develop strategy.
Adopt strategy.

Use the techniques and work in the ways which have been selected to clarify ends and develop alternative means of achieving these ends. Group and evaluate the means in order to choose a strategy.

E *Decide on plan format and implementation*

Agree on plan format.
Decide how it is to be implemented.

A strategic plan is a complex document and the form in which it is to be produced and used needs forethought. With some agreement on format all contributors know what the document should look like and a first draft can be produced. How the plan will be used in implementation and who will be involved in implementation needs discussion.

F *Plan and Implement*

Develop a first draft.
Refine the plan.
Adopt the plan.
Implement the plan.
Monitor performance.
Take corrective action.
Update the plan.

The plan needs refining through discussion and the final plan needs to be formally agreed and adopted. The plan should have actions, time-scales, resources required, staff development needs, and responsibilities incorporated so that a schedule of action is clear. As these actions are implemented they should be monitored and compared with the plan so that any corrective action can be taken. Periodically the plan should be updated.

Model 2 – Fidler and Bowles model

A model to indicate stages of strategic management in schools which supplements the Johnson and Scholes (1993) model is shown as Figure 12.3 (Fidler, Bowles with Hart 1991). This model shows the cyclic nature of strategic planning with the evaluation process at the end of one cycle feeding into the analysis stage of the next cycle. This model brings out two important differences from school development planning which has a similar cycle. At the analysis stage there are inputs from outside the school. These are illustrated in the model as market research by which the views of parents and potential parents about the school's operations are sought, and environmental scanning. This is the process by which influences outside the school which might affect its future are identified and assessed, particularly those which are growing in importance. This includes such influences as new requirements from central government and other statutory bodies but also includes more pervasive influences such as the possibilities of increased use of information technology. This vital process is further elaborated in Fidler et al. (1996).

The second major difference compared to school development planning shown on this diagram is the presence of a creative vision of the future in addition to the results of the analysis of the present, such that both inform possible choices for the future. From these a strategy is chosen to begin the transformation towards the vision.

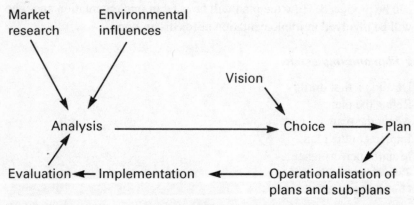

Figure 12.3. Fidler and Bowles Model – Evaluation, Vision, Choice, Operationalisation, Implementation

In particular this model elaborates the planning process to show the need to have broad plans which contain long-term trends and also more precise operating or action plans. The school will have a *mission* statement which gives its long-term purpose and the groups which it intends to serve and which have been questioned as part of the strategic analysis. In addition, the strategic plan will involve the creation of a short, compact, memorable, meaningful *focus statement* outlining the specific development of the school which this strategy encapsulates. The wording of this statement should have been refined to be as concise as possible whilst retaining as many of the nuances as possible which are the keys to the direction of many other aspects of the school's work. It should be capable of being 'unpacked' to yield the core values of the school and its vision of the future. The most basic feature of the statement is that it should be a *guide to action*. The strategic plan should have implications for each of a series of more detailed sub-plans. It should include implications for both what to do and also what not to do. In short, it should indicate (implicit) priorities.

The focus statement may be amplified by lists of long-term objectives which indicate intended progress on a range of fronts. These should be consistent with each other and where there are potential internal inconsistencies, the means by which these are to be resolved should be indicated.

The first level of detail of the strategic plan is the plan of the organisational structure and decision-making machinery of the school including the involvement of governors. The strategic plan will have implications for the structure of responsibilities in the school and that combined with the culture of the school will have implications for how decisions are made and the involvement of governors. Where this implies a change in the culture of the school, this should have been recognised at the choice stage and the extent of the implications of the change recognised.

The detailed sub-plans for the four main areas of decision-making in the school are:

Curriculum (and pupil outcomes) plan – what we intend to contribute to children's learning.
Staffing plan – how we intend to recruit and develop people with the skills to do it.
Financial (and material resources and premises) plan – how we intend to spend the money to help us achieve it.
Marketing plan – how we intend to obtain the resources and support and commitment of others to enable us to do it.

Each of these plans will be interrelated and consistent with the overall strategic plan. In each there will be long-term and short-term objectives. For example, in the staffing plan there might be a long-term aim to move to a more balanced age-profile of staff, to take on more classroom assistants and to take on more part-time teaching staff as a way of giving enhanced flexibility in the future and as part of a longer-term plan to make full-time teachers curriculum managers, and changing their role to planners and managers of learning.

Depending on finances, some limited progress on some of these may be possible but until some full-time teachers leave by promotion, retirements or other reason no major progress may be possible. However, the purpose of this aspect of the plan is to keep these issues in mind for the occasion when a full-time teacher leaves – 'Fortune favours the prepared mind' (Louis Pasteur).

The shorter-term objectives will find their expression in action plans including plans for parts of the school such as departments or teams. Thus there is a hierarchy of plans:

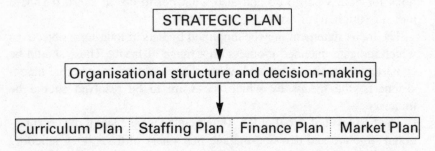

Although there are many differences between school development planning and strategic planning (Fidler, Bowles with Hart 1991), the most fundamental features which distinguish strategic planning from school development planning are that it:

– questions the aims of the school
– investigates the strategic standing of the school
– takes account of present and future environmental influences
– incorporates a vision of what the school should be like
– plans for the longer-term
– is holistic.

For some writers school development planning requires a collegial mode of operation. Strategic planning makes no such requirement. Most of the information on which to plan strategy may be held by senior management and so could be done by them, but at the functional level others may have valuable facts and opinions to contribute to the formulation of strategy and at the very least others in the organisation need to understand the strategy so that they can play their part within it. Although the process needs to be steered by the senior management of the schools, the wider involvement of all staff is advantageous. Thus strategy can be formulated either consultatively or participatively. Where it is formulated in a consultative way there will be a need to convince members of the organisation of the appropriateness of the strategy when formulated and to communicate with them about how implementing the strategy will involve them.

Whilst strategy is influenced by a vision of what might be, this is tempered by an assessment of current and future likely resources to make the vision sustainable. This is the managerial dimension.

There are a number of tensions within strategy:

1. It is based on a vision but it has to be sustainable.
2. It combines evaluation of the present with a vision of the future.
3. It takes account of the environment but tries to influence it.
4. It tries to combine the advantages of the stability provided by a plan with flexibility if the circumstances validating the plan change.

Whilst commercial interpretations of strategy start from competition and the need to stay ahead of competitors or find a market niche, in public service particularly, it can also start from the need to provide a high quality service to clients. Hence there is a need to know what clients think of the service and their future requirements. Having decided on a sustainable strategy there is then a need to tell clients and potential clients about the services offered and to be offered. Thus all the attributes of marketing are required but with a rationale which does not begin with competition.

Conclusion

School development planning provides a process which can be used to plan systematically and implement improvements in a school. It too needs to be treated as an innovation and its operation refined by reflecting on experience. That it needs to be done by the school primarily for its own benefit is absolutely clear. If it serves only or primarily the purposes of others it ceases to have value. What may have been underestimated by its advocates is the raising of morale which can be achieved by successfully accomplishing some improvement which was seen by staff in the school as an impediment to their success. From such a successful small start much more can be accomplished. My feeling is that this is more likely to be successful than attempting root innovations which have few tangible outcomes.

Success at school development planning alone is not enough to make the transition to strategic planning. At the heart of strategic planning is strategic thinking. This is the frame of mind that does not regard external

174

requirements as inevitable and inflexible, that has a view of how the organisation should be and seeks to use resources and circumstances to make improvements to move closer to the desired state of affairs. Strategic planning offers a more co-operative and systematic way of achieving this. However, it should be remembered that, all of this is but a means of achieving improved education for children and young people in schools.

CHAPTER THIRTEEN

Higher and Further Education Colleges: Approaches to Institutional Self-Review

by Frances Kelly

It would be misleading to suggest in this chapter that the ways in which the further and higher education sectors provide quality assurance offer models of ideal processes. Indeed the critical debate regarding quality assurance, particularly in higher education, has dominated the pages of the education press over the past three years.

However, two features which contrast significantly with the OFSTED inspection model are worth consideration. These are the role and importance of self-assessment by the institution as part of the external quality assessment, and the concept of assurance by peer review.

In this chapter I shall examine each of these, in relation to their impact on the accountability for performance within the sector, their ability to promote quality improvement and their current or possible use in schools. This leads then to a comparison of the models of assessment and audit.

The findings come from a current investigation into models of internal quality assurance in each sector of the education system, and a comparison of their relationships with the sectors' external quality monitoring systems.

The Higher Education Funding Council for England (HEFCE) and the Further Education Funding Council (FEFC) were established by the 1992 Further and Higher Education Act. This Act required each council to make provision for 'assessing the quality of education provided in institutions for whose activities it provides, or is considering providing, financial support'.

HEFCE assesses quality in each cognate (subject) area as a separate event. It uses a four stage method:

– self-assessment by the department

- assessment visit by academic peers
- assessment judgement
- assessment report.

FEFC retains an inspectorate but involves a large number of part-time inspectors drawn from the FE colleges. Its inspection process separates out curriculum areas from a number of cross-college provisions (such as governance and management and including quality assurance). Each aspect is graded separately and the FEFC insist that it is inappropriate to aggregate grades to the College level. The inspection procedure requires colleges to provide a self-assessment based on the evidence of their own quality assurance procedures.

Self-assessment

Higher education

Studies of external quality assessment processes in higher education throughout Western Europe, and North America (Brennan and van Vugt 1993) show a wide acceptance of the importance of basing quality assessment on institutional self-assessment, and this is at the heart of the HEFCE quality assessment process. For most institutions it externalises the process of course and departmental reviews which have existed as internal procedures for some time. Those institutions which used to offer qualifications validated by the Council for National Academic Awards (CNNA) were required to show evidence that they regularly reviewed their own practices, and monitored their performance, while for the older universities the exercise of self-criticism was a key element in the definition of a university, although the concept of an external body carrying out assessments on a national basis was not. A study of the universities where good practice in self-assessment had been identified showed a common pattern of review.

Each year the teaching team for each course must submit a course review of the curriculum, the teaching and learning strategies employed, the assessment procedures and their results, and the students' experiences. The report is based on data collected by staff, from students through meetings and questionnaires and from the report of the external examiner.

Every five years a departmental review is held, where a critical analysis of the performance of the department over the previous five years and its plans for future development is tested by a review team made up of internal and external academic peers (and often non-academics with appropriate professional or industrial experience). While the department generally nominates appropriate members for the review team, supported by evidence of their expertise, the final selection is made by the Academic Board of the University.

The universities have in place a variety of mechanisms to ensure that the departmental reviews are rigorous and require ongoing evidence through the course reviews that the plans are being implemented.

The procedure used by HEFCE is an extension of the five-yearly review. The reviewers are external academics nominated by their own universities and selected and trained by the Funding Council. They receive a self-assessment document prepared by the department being assessed looking at the following issues:

- Curriculum design, content and organisation
- Teaching, learning and assessment
- Student progression and achievement
- Student support and guidance
- Learning resources
- Quality assurance and enhancement.

In each area broad indications of the issues that should be addressed by each department in preparing its self-assessment are provided.

At first for many institutions self-assessment was the whole of the process. Departments could choose to bid for 'excellent' status, and would then receive an assessment visit, but for those departments which chose to submit the self-assessment as satisfactory, only a random sample of assessment visits were conducted.

A review held 12 months after the introduction of the assessments however reported considerable dissatisfaction with this practice among the institutions, and confirmed that the assessment visit had a significant impact on how effective the preparation of the self-assessment was in terms of developing an internal culture of quality enhancement. While two thirds of the visited departments felt that the process of developing the self-assessment report had produced benefits to their departments, only 40 per cent of non-visited departments reported such positive views (Barnett et al. 1994).

From April 1995 the proposed new procedures mean that all departments will be visited. It is predicted that this will double the cost of assessment.

More importantly there was evidence that the self-assessments lacked critical appraisal and analysis, being instead simply a description of the department and its practices. Departments are in a difficult position here. If the tone of the self-assessment is genuinely self-critical there is a risk that, having exposed its weaknesses on record, this exposure could be used against the department, particularly given that the quality assessment is being conducted by the Funding Council, and one of its stated aims is to inform funding.

The pressure exists therefore to make the self-assessment serve a public relations function and operate from an optimistic rather than a realistic viewpoint. Such a process however makes the exercise of limited value to the institutions or to their students.

The proposed solution HEFCE has offered to this is to make the quality and rigour of the self-assessment itself part of the whole assessment exercise. So a self-assessment which is deemed to be insufficiently analytical, and which fails to show evidence of a self-critical approach or to identify areas for development will be criticised for this in the public report produced at the end of the assessment process.

The role of the assessment visit is primarily intended to test the rigour of the self-assessment and the extent to which it presents an accurate picture of the quality of the education that students in the subject receive. The self-assessment informs and shapes the activities of the assessment team, but assessors do have the freedom to develop lines of inquiry in the light of evidence gathered as the assessment visit proceeds.

Further education

The further education inspection process recognises the importance of institutions developing their own quality assurance practices. In *Assessing Achievement*, the Council's inspection framework, it requires that colleges submit 'the findings of the college's own quality assurance procedures as expressed in an internal quality assessment report' as one of the four elements of documentary evidence prior to the inspection. In addition quality assurance is one of the five cross-college aspects of provision which are graded in the published reports.

While recognising that at that time some colleges were only beginning to develop internal quality assurance systems, the Council required that by the 1994/95 academic year this report should 'state, and provide supporting evidence for, the college's own assessment of its strengths and weaknesses as a basis for discussion with the inspection team'.

The areas to be covered in this assessment are:

- responsiveness and range of provision
- governance and management
- students' recruitment, guidance and support
- teaching and the promotion of learning
- students' achievements
- quality assurance
- resources:
  staffing

equipment and learning resources
accommodation.

The FEFC Inspection Unit is currently examining the self-assessment reports received to date to identify common elements and to assess their rigour and validity as against the reports produced by the inspection team.

Analysis of the external inspection reports published by the Council indicates that where good practice in quality assurance has been identified, colleges have developed internal systems to monitor the development of new programmes and courses, and to ensure that regular course reviews occur and are acted on. The course reviews include input from the teaching teams, from students, from employers, and where applicable from external moderators, and lead to documented plans for improvement at course level. This model closely resembles the university annual course review exercise. There is not, however, evidence of programmes of wider departmental reviews to the same degree.

An evaluation questionnaire is provided to each college at the conclusion of the inspection. The Council's findings from these indicate that one of the most positive aspects of the inspection process is its encouragement to teachers in the development of self-assessment skills.

Schools

The practice of self-assessment in schools has existed as part of the school development planning process for some time. A variety of models for self-assessment have been produced, and a number of local education authorities have provided considerable training for staff in carrying out audit and evaluation within the schools.

In schools where good practice in development planning has been identified, regular reviews of departments, following very similar lines to those in other sectors, occur. The department (either as a curriculum area or an age grouping) provides an analysis of its own performance which is verified by a review team.

The analysis may be based on the GRIDS framework, or may use ethos indicators, or a process developed within a Local Education Authority. It will include data from external and internal pupil assessments, a staff review of curriculum, teaching and learning strategies, staff development and resource use, and increasingly will include the views of both pupils and their parents. An integral part of the analysis is the preparation of the Development Plan which addresses the issues identified by the department.

The review team usually includes the head teacher, and/or deputies, a member of the governing body and an appropriate external subject specialist. Some schools are trying also to involve heads of departments as reviewers of departments other than their own to encourage the spread of good practice.

The team spends time both observing classes and in discussion groups with the teachers and pupils. Importantly their role is not to carry out the assessment, but to check that the department's own analysis is accurate and that the Development Plan addresses the core issues in a sufficiently rigorous manner. They are able to do this in the context of the school's own culture and ethos, and because the Development Plan which emerges stems from the department's own analysis, it is significantly owned by the department's staff.

The current practice of OFSTED however appears to undervalue the experiences of schools in this area, although the revised *Framework* to be introduced in 1996 may give more prominence to self-evaluation. While a great amount of raw statistical data is required from the school prior to the inspection visit, it is the inspectorate's role to analyse this data and carry out the assessment. The head teacher is invited to make a brief statement about the school but this does not carry through to the departmental level.

Further, while the School Development Plan is one element of the documentation to be provided to the inspection team, there would appear to be no policy in the framework for inspection for its appraisal, either in terms of its content (except in relationship to budgeting) or the process by which it was developed. In the two sample inspection reports included in the *Framework* handbook, the School Development Plan receives only one reference – under the heading of 'Efficiency of the school' in relation to budgeting.

One of the key issues raised by current research into the OFSTED process is the conflict which occurs when the Action Plan required following the OFSTED report conflicts with the Development Plan prepared by the school. To require that priority be given to the Action Plan undermines the role of the governors and staff of the school as local managers, and encourages the view of the individual school as a franchise outlet, dispensing a nationally set curriculum according to the model defined by OFSTED.

Alternatively the OFSTED Action Plan is perceived as 'peripheral' to the School Development Plan, because the issues it requires the school to address are not owned by the school itself. Indeed the comment has been made regarding some issues that while they were required to be addressed in the Action Plan, the school had no intention of progressing them further than the paper document.

Practices in both higher and further education attempt to minimise this conflict by integrating the institution's self-assessment into the external quality assessment process, and by focusing on the development of more rigorous practices by the institutions themselves. In the detail published by OFSTED in its *Handbook,* schools are provided with a model for self-assessment which could be internalised. In some local education authorities a comparative analysis of the *Handbook* requirements and the LEA's own school development evaluation process is being conducted with a view to integrate the two. However, it should be noted that if the model set out in the *Handbook* was to be prescribed for all schools' self-assessment, there would need to be considerable debate regarding the definitions of quality and of education implicit in it.

Peer review

HEFCE relies on universities releasing academic staff to act as assessors in their subject areas. Indeed the system is best described as peer review of the self-assessment. When complaints were made regarding the quality and suitability of some assessors, HEFCE was able to place these back with the universities for solution on the grounds that the great majority were their nominees.

The value to both an individual and an institution of an academic taking part in the assessment or audit of another institution is considerable both in terms of the individual staff development opportunities offered, and the development of critical capability for the institution.

The training provided for assessors focuses on developing the skills required to conduct an evaluation of a subject area with sensitivity to the aims and objectives of the provider, rather than those of the assessor, and familiarity with the assessment method to be used. In this it can build on the experience of the academic in the processes of course and departmental review.

In the further education system the inspection team is large. Three key features of the make-up of the team deserve particular comment.

Firstly, the inspection programme is established by a full-time inspector who is assigned to the college on a long term basis, and is also responsible for building up an in depth knowledge of the college and its local context, and monitoring its responses following the inspection. In this he or she carries out the role of the Link Inspector in a local authority. While strictly speaking this person is not a 'peer', the liaison role promotes an ongoing relationship between the inspectorate and the college.

Secondly, the college is invited to nominate a senior member of staff to participate as a member of the inspection team. All but one of the FE colleges inspected in 1993–94 chose to take advantage of this invitation.

The staff nominee is briefed by the Inspection unit for their role, and is able to take part in all aspects of the inspection, but does not contribute to decisions on quality grades allocated to departments or across the college.

The particular value of this practice is that it increases the ability of the inspection team to relate to the culture of the college, and to interpret the evidence provided. A further benefit is to increase the ownership by the college of the findings of the inspection because the staff nominee has been a part of the process.

Thirdly, a significant number of the inspectors are part-time inspectors, who work normally in further education, generally as heads of departments or in management of a broader aspect of a college's work. Following their course of training, each is required to make two supervised inspection visits, one focused on their specialist area, and the other looking at performance in inspection of cross-college provisions. For these visits the trainee is required to plan the process, carry out the examination of documents, interview staff, observe teaching, assess students' achievements and prepare a written report of the inspection.

The value here lies both in the experiences which the part-time inspector can take back to his or her own institution, in terms of the practices of the inspection service and the standards and practices operating in other institutions, and in the experience for the institutions which offer themselves for a training inspection as an intermediate step between their internal reviews and the formal FEFC inspection.

As in higher education, therefore, the quality of the inspectorate is very dependent on the willingness of institutions to release appropriate staff. Feedback from people working in the sector suggests that a significant number of colleges have recognised the value not only to the individual and the institution in terms of expertise, but also to the sector as a whole in developing an inspectorate which has the respect and confidence of the sector and of those to whom it provides accountability.

Recent statements from OFSTED indicate that they intend to explore the use of heads and senior teachers as part-time OFSTED inspectors, following appropriate training.

These three factors (the liaison inspector, the staff nominee inspector, and the use of part-time peer inspectors) together have been a significant feature in the further education inspection framework gaining acceptance from the FE colleges, and, it is believed, in effecting quality enhancement as an integral part of the inspection process.

These models differ considerably from the current OFSTED practice of inspection by a team which is required to be made up of inspectors who have no major connections with the school.

This raises the questions of whether quality improvement can better be achieved through integrating the inspection process with the quality improvement culture of the institution itself or by seeing it solely as an external judgement, and whether it is solely accountability which is provided by the snapshot judgement of practice within the short time-frame of an inspection visit, and supported by raw statistical data.

Assessment or audit

Within the higher education system a further external quality monitoring process is provided by the Higher Education Quality Council (HEQC). This body was established by the higher education institutions themselves to contribute to the maintenance and improvement of quality. It offers a regular quality audit service for institutions.

A quality audit looks at how the university provides its own quality assurance. The university prepares briefing documentation which describes and illustrates the ways in which it assures quality. This covers such areas as how it develops and approves new courses and programmes, and regularly reviews those in place, how it monitors the teaching, learning and communication methods used, how student assessment is carried out to ensure it is valid and reliable, and how the university ensures that its promotional material is not misleading.

Once again this material is presented in the form of a self-assessment, indicating strengths and weaknesses identified by the institution. This documentation is studied by a group of auditors, once again using peers drawn from other institutions and trained by HEQC. An audit visit occurs during which the auditors meet with staff and students, individually and in groups, to verify that there is widespread knowledge and use of the procedures the university described in its briefing documentation, and an audit report is prepared, describing the quality assurance processes which the audit team was able to confirm were in place, giving their perception of the effectiveness of those processes, and commenting both on areas of good practice and areas which should be considered for improvement.

The audit unit uses a series of simple questions in its analysis. It asks the university to explain:

- what is the university trying to do to assure its quality
- why is it trying to do these particular things
- how is it doing them
- why did it chose to operate in this particular way
- why does it think the way it has chosen is the best way of assuring quality
- how does it know that its procedures work

– how does it go about improving its quality assurance.

Thus the audit is not making an external assessment of the quality of the provision of the programmes as such, but is looking at how the university itself performs that assessment function on a regular basis, and, importantly, how it ensures that improvements take place.

This distinction is a critical one because it recognises that institutions in higher education are fully self-managing and that setting and maintaining academic standards is a fundamental aspect of self-management.

While the situation for schools has significant differences, in terms of the role of the National Curriculum and the student assessment procedures associated with it, the model of quality audit promotes a positive culture of regular self-evaluation and improvement.

The Quality Council regularly analyses its reports and publishes a general account of good practice compiled from its audits, naming the specific universities where the practice can be observed. This provides a valuable resource for universities looking to improve some aspect of their procedures. A similar model exists for schools in the Strathclyde area where the Education Authority's Quality Assurance Unit publishes annual bulletins of good practice observed in its inspections, naming the schools concerned.

Conclusions

Practices in both the further and higher education sectors indicate that while self-assessment on its own cannot provide a valid measure for accountability, it is an extremely important factor in quality improvement.

The issues raised in this chapter are not merely of academic interest. An A-level programme may be offered at a College of Further Education, a Sixth Form College, a consortium of secondary schools or at a single school. The current range of external quality assessment procedures gives different levels of responsibility for quality assurance to the teacher, depending on the institution in which the programme is offered. Further comparative studies of the models of external assessment to determine the most effective way to provide accountability while fostering institutional quality improvement would have considerable value.

If a school's self-assessment has been sufficiently rigorous, then the inspection process will become one of sampling the evidence to test the validity of the self-assessment, and not a repetition of the self-assessment. The length of the external inspection cycle means that a school can expect to be inspected only once during the time of any single pupil's attendance. For improvement to occur a culture of critical self-examination on a much more regular basis would be of greater value.

An effective way to develop the ability of an institution to be self-critical is to provide for individual staff members to act as reviewers both within their own schools, and as peers for others.

In *The Audit Explosion* Michael Power (1994) makes the point that society currently runs the risk of transferring responsibility for performance from the individual performing a role to those who audit their performance. In our terms responsibility for the quality of education would then lie not with the teachers and the schools, but with the Office which inspects their performance. The corollary of this means that a further set of auditors are required for the first line of auditors and so on in a line to ensure accountability. Power suggests that society would be better served by placing responsibility for assuring quality at the chalk face.

In common with schools, the higher education and further education sectors currently face many difficulties in reconciling the maintenance and improvement of quality with constantly reduced funding. While many flaws have been identified in their practices of quality assessment, I have highlighted a number of areas where the practice in these sectors has something to offer to the statutory sector.

CHAPTER FOURTEEN

School Development, School Inspection and Managing Change

by Brian Fidler, Peter Earley and Janet Ouston

The contributors to this book have had as their main focus school development and school improvement and a variety of approaches and strategies, including that of external audit, have been explored and critiques offered. Our definition of school improvement follows that given in the International School Improvement Programme which defined it as:

> ... a systematic, sustained effort aimed at change in learning conditions and other related internal conditions in one or more schools, *with the ultimate aim of accomplishing educational goals more effectively.* (Miles and Ekholm 1985, p48). (Our emphasis.)

For Hopkins and colleagues school improvement is:

> ... a distinct approach to educational change that enhances student outcomes as well as strengthening the school's capacity for managing change. (Hopkins, Ainscow and West 1994)

Our assumption is that the impetus for change is manifested at the *school level.* The pressure for change may lie outside the school but it is the realisation of a need to change and a commitment to change which must come from the school itself. For schools to achieve meaningful change and improvement, the school itself needs to be in the driving seat with the head teacher providing the necessary leadership. Heads cannot plan and manage successful change alone but should lead and see themselves responsible for change. Changes emanating from within the school itself need encouragement and support from the head and the senior management team.

Where heads and schools are in this position then the need is for skills and assistance to achieve change. Any help needs to be employed by the school so that it has a *direct* stake in choosing and working with any consultant or purchasing any technical assistance.

External audits, such as those currently undertaken by OFSTED, provide schools with a baseline from which they can look to future improvement. Whether or not this mode of audit represents 'value for money' or is particularly cost-effective in facilitating school improvement is debatable (for example, see Hargreaves 1995a). However, OFSTED claims that inspection provides an objective account of 'where the school is and where it might go in the future'. More specifically the value of OFSTED inspections are three-fold. They:

(a) Provide schools with an incentive to develop in preparation for inspection.
(b) Offer an outside audit and list of points for action.
(c) Can point out the lack of the two crucial preconditions for improvement:
    (i) a head teacher capable of giving leadership, and
    (ii) a school with the skills and confidence to respond. Where the first is absent action will need to be taken by others to institute the conditions for improvement.

Any innovation should directly or indirectly improve the learning of children in schools. Schools should plan improvements to meet their own problems and to address their own agendas. They should avoid 'fadism' and, where possible, also ensure that the success of the innovation has been successfully evaluated elsewhere before taking it up.

Any of the innovations and approaches described in the earlier chapters – competences or Standards (whether individual or organisational), Organisational Development, Total Quality Management or continuous improvement – need first and foremost to be treated as *changes*. However worthy they are as initiatives, they are unlikely to receive universal acclaim and even if they did their introduction would need rational planning. Their introduction will also need to take account of the prevailing culture and the micropolitics of the organisation.

Where leadership is committed to improvement, the skills and techniques needed are those of *planned change*. These are the range of techniques for transition management taken over from organisational development or OD (Beckhard and Harris 1987; Everard and Morris 1990; Fidler, Bowles with Hart 1991). These examine the staff for readiness for change, capability for change, forces for and against change, and commitment to change. A consideration of change by the exertion of power, rational argument or persuasion (Chin and Benne 1976) will help clarify complementary approaches to change.

The starting point for change is the unfreezing process (Lewin 1951). People need to feel dissatisfied with the present before they are likely to be ready for change. Institutional self-review or other means of discovering areas of the school's work which are not operating well should be instituted. Attempting to bring about change before people are psychologically ready is unlikely to be successful, particularly in the case of sustained or major change.

Having 'unfrozen' the present situation a change can be contemplated. This can either involve single loop learning (doing present things better) or double loop learning (doing different things) (Argyris and Schön 1987). Self-review or an external inspection by OFSTED is likely to induce single loop learning since it will be based on improving present operations. Only some kind of vision of a better future is likely to induce double loop learning.

Development planning should itself be seen as a development which needs to be worked at (Constable 1994). As Constable (Constable, Norton and Abbott 1991) has pointed out, mere increased experience of development planning will not necessarily improve development planning. It needs active refection on the process and its successes and failures to help get better. Development planning is a meta-development in its own right. A particular irony of learning from long-term developments like this is that we seldom experience the consequences from which to learn (Sengé 1990).

School improvement needs both *leadership* and *good management* (Fidler 1996). Here leadership is reserved for processes such as forging new ideas, consulting and persuading others, and making symbolic acts which inspire and give meaning to others. This inspirational component needs to be supplemented with the planning, staffing, resourcing, etc. of good management which is capable of getting results once the direction has been set.

Any attempt to move from the reactive to the proactive needs to be accompanied by a change to *strategic management*. It is necessary to try to predict future influences and possibilities and to weigh up external requirements rather than just accepting them (Fidler et al. 1996).

Attempts to change need to take account of the prevailing *culture* of the school – 'the way we do things around here' – the taken for granted assumptions about how people in this school go about their business. Culture both restricts the possible options that may be considered and even the perceptions of participants, as well as setting the parameters for decision-making (Schein 1992). It also provides a powerful limitation on change. Any attempt to institutionalise the change – or refreeze in Lewin's terms – means an incorporation into the culture. Everyone pays lip service to the difficulty of changing the culture but in practice overlooks these and just assumes good ideas will stick (Fidler et al. 1996).

Any attempt to change a school has to be individually tailored to where the school is in terms of its previous history of development and its problems. Any improvement has to be seen to address the school's perceived problems rather than some external group's agenda, however worthy. The start has to be on what are pressing problems for the school. Similarly, strategies for school improvement will need to be differentiated depending on the school and its cultural and situational context.

There is a need for caution when entering into any large scale, whole-school innovation without the wholehearted and considerable support of the majority of staff. For other innovations this may be less severe but without widespread support, initiatives such as 'Investors in People' and competence-based approaches will be less likely to be successful. People will 'go through the motions' and wait for them to be forgotten or overtaken by the next fad. There is much history of this in education and we must begin to learn from experience.

Most accounts of development planning and school improvement do not involve any consideration of conflict. There is the assumption of collegiality (contrived or not) with its emphasis on consensus and partnerships. There may be no open or obvious 'stand up' rows within the organisation but is it wise to assume that passive resistance is any the less conflict? Conflict and resistance needs to be faced and successfully resolved (Schmuck and Runkel 1985; Everard and Morris 1990).

A culture of self-improvement or *organisational learning* (Swieringa and Wierdsma 1992) would appear to be one which has a lot to offer. This is learning over and above the learning of each individual. It involves co-operation and a commitment to solve problems together. It also needs a concentration on the learning process. Pilots will not always be successful but experimentation has to be fostered. It will be interesting to see the extent to which initiatives such as 'Investors in People' are able to help schools become 'learning organisations' in this sense.

To show the importance of improvement and to tempt schools to take part in developmental initiatives, extra resources probably need to be made available. Perhaps these should be made available as a result of a bidding process by which schools have to formulate a need. There should be a requirement for monitoring reports to show that the resources are being committed in accordance with the bid and an evaluation before further resources are released. Recent changes to enable GEST funds to be more closely linked to OFSTED's 'key issues for action' is a recognition of the need to 'oil the wheels of change'.

There needs to be a change in the culture of schools to make the use of *consultants* the norm rather than exceptional. Schools need the resources to use consultants but, as some of the contributors to this book have noted, they also need to learn how to make good use of them. Appropriately skilled consultants are also needed.

Three types of consultancy have been identified and these have been outlined by Morris (1988):

Directive – the consultant focuses on the organisation's measures of success, identifies reasons for shortcomings and recommends changes in personnel, structure and methods to improve. The consultant may be further commissioned to implement the suggestions.

Behavioural – the consultant's role is to develop the people in the organisation to handle their relationships and conflicts. They will normally be trained in group dynamics and other behavioural techniques.

Catalytic – the consultant helps the people to focus on organisational performance and assists them to identify and put into practice ways of improving performance. There will be some training in behavioural techniques and management skills training in functional areas in addition to workshops where people work directly on the organisation's problems and formulate action plans.

Those with a concern for relationships may be termed *process* consultants, whilst both the behavioural and the catalytic are 'capacity-building functions' (Louis 1981). For Everard (1988) a process consultant is someone who is:

- outside the management of the school
- in the workplace but not of it (i.e. intentionally marginal)
- politically neutral (though not unaware)
- facilitating and educating about the process of organizational problem-solving
- client-oriented
- problem-oriented (rather than activity-oriented).

Murgatroyd (1988) has pointed out that any consultant needs an explicit *theory of organisations* rather than just experience. Without such a theory the consultant is unlikely to be able to facilitate successful organisational change. Consultants need this if they are to be able to compare the workings of one school with another in a meaningful way.

The issue of the involvement of staff – all staff – in school development is worthy of further consideration. Is there a need for full and active consultation on all matters? Probably full consultation and support is the best combination along with school leadership which people trust and believe in. There is no evidence that in a participatory system teachers will necessarily agree to do what is in the best interests of the children rather than their own interests, no matter how well this is rationalised. The head teacher, along with the governing body, is there above all to promote the interests of children.

'Crisis ridden' schools need an appraisal of leadership and then assistance when this has been resolved. 'Complacent' schools need a stimulus (support) and some badgering (pressure) but those schools who want to improve should be given the skills and (ongoing) training and some consultancy but left to develop their own strategies for improvement. In this way opportunities for meaningful change and development are likely to be enhanced with concomitant benefits for both students and staff.

Appendix

The 24 assessment indicators used in the *Investors in People* national Standard are under four headings:

Commitment

1.1 There is a public commitment from the most senior level within the organisation to develop people.

1.2 Employees at all levels are aware of the broad aims or vision of the organisation.

1.3 There is a written but flexible plan which sets out business goals and targets.

1.4 The plan identifies broad development needs and specifies how they will be met.

1.5 The employer has considered what employees at all levels will contribute to the success of the organisation and has communicated this effectively to them.

1.6 Where representative structures exist, management communicates with employee representatives a vision of where the organisation is going and the contribution employees (and their representatives) will make to its success.

Planning

2.1 The written plan identifies the resources that will be used to meet training and development needs.

2.2 Training and development needs are regularly reviewed against business objectives.

2.3 A process exists for regularly reviewing the training and development needs of all employees.

2.4 Responsibility for developing people is clearly identified throughout the organisation, starting at the top.

2.5 Managers are competent to carry out their responsibilities for developing people.

2.6 Targets and standards are set for development actions.

2.7 Where appropriate, training targets are linked to achieving external standards, and particularly to NVQs (a kind of accreditation being encouraged by the government).

Action

3.1 All new employees are introduced effectively to the organisation and are given the training and development they need to do their job.
3.2 The skills of existing employees are developed in line with business objectives.
3.3 All employees are made aware of the development opportunities open to them.
3.4 All employees are encouraged to help identify and meet their job-related development needs.
3.5 Effective action takes place to achieve the training and development objectives of individuals and the organisation.
3.6 Managers are actively involved in supporting employees to meet their training and development needs.

Evaluation

4.1 The organisation evaluates how its development of people is contributing to business goals and targets.
4.2 The organisation evaluates whether its development actions have achieved their objectives.
4.3 The outcomes of training and development are evaluated at individual, team and organisational levels.
4.4 Top management understand the broad costs and benefits of developing people.
4.5 The continuing commitment of top management to developing people is communicated to all employees.

References

Abbott, J. (1994) *Learning makes sense*. Letchworth: Education 2000.

Aguayo, R. (1990) *Dr. Deming: The Man who taught the Japanese about Quality*. London: Mercury.

Argyris, C. and Schön, D. (1987) *Organizational Learning: A Theory of Action Perspective* (Second Edition). Reading, Mass.: Addison-Wesley.

Audit Commission (1989) *Losing an Empire, Finding a Role: The LEA of the Future*. Occasional Paper, 10. London: HMSO.

Baginsky, M., Baker, L. and Cleave, S. (1991) *Towards Effective Partnerships in School Governance*. Slough: NFER.

Barber, M., Denning, T., Gough, G. and Johnson, M. (1995) *Urban Education Initiatives: The National Pattern*. London: OFSTED.

Barnett, R. et al. (1994) *Assessment of the Quality of Higher Education: A Review and an Evaluation*. Bristol: HEFCE.

Barry, B. (1986) *Strategic Planning Workbook for Nonprofit Organizations*. St Paul, Minn.: Amherst H Wilder Foundation.

Barth, R. (1986) 'On sheep and goats and educational reform', *Phi Delta Kappa*, **68**(4) 293–6.

Barth, R. (1993) 'Raising achievement in the inner city'. Paper presented at the Haggerston Conference, Haggerston School, London.

Beckhard, R. and Harris, R. (1987) *Organizational Transitions: Managing Complex Change* (Second Edition). Reading, Mass.: Addison-Wesley.

Bernstein, B. (1970) 'Education cannot compensate for society', *New Society*, 387, 344–7.

Biott, C., Easen, P. and Atkins, M. (1994) 'Written planning and school development: biding time or making time?', in Hargreaves, D. and Hopkins, D. (eds) *Development Planning for School Improvement*. London: Cassell.

Block, P. (1981) *Flawless Consulting*. San Diego: University Associates.

Bolam, R., McMahon, A., Pocklington, K. and Weindling, D. (1993) *Effective Management in Schools*. London: HMSO.

Brennan, J. and van Vugt, F. (1993) *Questions of Quality in Europe and Beyond*. Milton Keynes: Quality Support Centre, Open University.

Brown, S., Duffield, J. and Riddell, S. (1995) 'School effectiveness research: the policy makers' tool for school improvement?', *European Educational Research Association Bulletin*, **1**(1), 6–15.

Bryson, J. (1988) *Strategic Planning for Public and Nonprofit Organizations: A Guide to Strengthening and Sustaining Organizational Achievement*. San Francisco: Jossey-Bass.

Burgess, T. (ed.) (1992) *Accountability in Schools*. Harlow: Longman.

Chin, R. and Benne, K. (1976) 'General strategies for effecting changes in human systems', in Bennis, W. et al. (eds) *The Planning of Change*. New York: Holt, Rinehart & Winston.

Clift, P. (1982) 'LEA schemes for school self-evaluation: a critique', *Educational Research*, **24**(4), 262–71.

Clift, P. (1987) 'School-based review: a response from the UK', in Hopkins, D. (ed.) *Improving the Quality of Schooling: Lessons from the OECD International School Improvement Project*. Lewes: Falmer Press.

Coleman, P. and LaRocque, L. (1990) *Struggling to be 'Good Enough': Administrative Practices and School District Ethos*. New York: Falmer Press.

Constable, H., Norton, J. and Abbott, I. (1991) *Case Studies in School Development Planning*. Sunderland: Sunderland Polytechnic School of Education.

Constable, H. (1994) 'Three arenas of tension; teachers' experience of participation in school development planning', in Hargreaves, D. and Hopkins, D. (eds) *Development Planning for School Improvement*. London: Cassell.

Corey, S. (1953) *Action Research to Improve School Practices*. New York: Columbia University.

Corrick, M. (1995) 'Effective governing bodies?', *Governors' Action*, Issue 35. Coventry: Action for Governors' Information and Training.

Costa, A.L. and Kallick, B. (1993) 'Through the lens of a critical friend', *Educational Leadership*, **51**(2), 49–51.

Creese, M. (1994) *Inspecting the Governors*. Bury St Edmunds: School Management and Governance Development.

Dalin, P. and Rolff, H. (1993) *Changing the School Culture*. London: Cassell/IMTEC.

Dalin, P. and Rust, V. (1983) *Can Schools Change?* Windsor: NFER–Nelson.

Deming, W. (1986) *Out of the Crisis*. Cambridge, Mass.: MIT.

Deming, W. (1993) *The New Economics for Industry, Government, Education*. Cambridge, Mass.: MIT.

Department of Education and Science (1989) *Planning for School Development: Advice to Governors, Headteachers and Teachers*. London: DES.

Department of Education and Science (1991) *Development Planning: A Practical Guide: Advice to Governors, Headteachers and Teachers*. London: DES.

Department for Education (DfE) (1994a) *School Governors: A Guide to the Law*. London: DfE.

Department for Education (DfE) (1994b) *Code of Practice on the Identification and Assessment of Special Educational Needs*. London: Central Office of Information.

Department for Education (DfE) (1995a) '*Effective Schools*'. Secretary of State's Speech to the Industrial Society Conference, Performance Management, 20 February. London, DfE *News*.

Department for Education (DfE) (1995b) *Governing Bodies and Effective Schools*. London: DfE.

Drucker, P. (1990) *Managing the Non-Profit Organisation*. Oxford: Butterworth-Heinemann.

Earley, P. (1992a) *The School Management Competences Project: Final Report*. Crawley: School Management South.

Earley, P. (1992b) *The School Management Competences Project: Standards for School Management*. Crawley: School Management South.

Earley, P. (1994) *School Governing Bodies: Making Progress?* Slough: NFER.

Earley, P. (1995) 'Managing our greatest resource: The evaluation of the Continuous Professional Development in Schools project'. Oxford: CBI Education Foundation.

Earley P., Fidler B. and Ouston J. (1995) 'OFSTED for more than accountability', *Management in Education*, **9**(1), 21–2.

Edwards, P., Denegri, D., Highfield, P. and Little, E. (1994) *Governor Training and Support in Hampshire*. Winchester: Educational Development Services for Hampshire County Council.

Egan, G. (1994) 'Re-engineering the company culture', *Management Today*, April.

Esp, D. (1993) *Competences for School Managers*. London: Kogan Page.

Everard, B. (1988) 'Training and consultancy: lessons from industry', in Gray, H. (ed.) *Management Consultancy in Schools*. London: Cassell.

Everard, B. and Morris, G. (1990) *Effective School Management*. London: Paul Chapman Publishing.

Fidler, B. (1989) 'Strategic management in schools', in Fidler, B. and Bowles, G. (eds) *Effective Local Management of Schools*. Harlow: Longman.

Fidler, B. (1992) 'Job descriptions and organisational structure', in Fidler, B. and Cooper, R. (eds) *Staff Appraisal and Staff Management in Schools and Colleges: A Guide to Implementation*. Harlow: Longman.

Fidler, B. (1996) 'The case for school leadership', in Watson, K. and Modgil, S. (eds) *Educational Dilemmas: Debate and Diversity* (Volume 3) *Power & Responsibility*. London: Cassell.

Fidler, B. and Bowles, G. with Hart, J. (1991) *Planning Your School's Strategy: ELMS Workbook*. Harlow: Longman.

Fidler, B., Earley, P. and Ouston, J. (1995) 'OFSTED school inspections and their impact on school development'. Paper presented to the British Educational Research Association, University of Bath, September.

Fidler, B. with Edwards, M., Evans, B., Mann, P. and Thomas, P. (1996) *Strategic Planning for School Improvement*. London: Pitman.

French, W. and Bell, C. (1984) *Organization Development* (Third Edition). Englewood Cliffs, NJ: Prentice Hall.

Fullan, M. (1982) *The Meaning of Educational Change*. Ontario: Teachers' College Press.

Fullan, M. (1991) *The New Meaning of Educational Change*. London: Cassell.

Fullan, M. (1992a) *Halton Model: Characteristics of Effective Schools*. Ontario: Halton Board of Education.

Fullan, M. (1992b) *What's Worth Fighting For in Headship*? Buckingham: Open University Press.

Fullan, M. (1993) *Change Forces: Probing the Depths of Educational Reform*. London: Falmer Press.

Fullan, M. and Hargreaves, A. (1992) *What's Worth Fighting For in Your School?* Buckingham: Open University Press.

Further Education Funding Council (1994) *An Evaluation of the Work of the Inspectorate 1993–1994*. London: FEFC.

Glover, D. (1990) 'Towards a school development plan: process and practice', *Educational Management and Administration*, **18**(3), 22–6.

Goddard, D. and Leask, M. (1992) *The Search for Quality: Planning for Improvement and Managing Change*. London: Paul Chapman Publishing.

Goldstein, H. (1987) *Multilevel Models in Educational and Social Research*. London: Griffin.

Goldstein, H. (1993) 'Assessment and accountability'. *Parliamentary Brief*, October, 33–4.

Goldstein, H. and Thomas, S. (1995) 'School effectiveness and 'value-added' analysis', *Forum*, **37**(2), 36–8.

Goldstein, H., Rasbash, J., Yang, M., Woodhouse, G., Pan, H., Nuttall, D. and Thomas, S. (1993) 'A multilevel analysis of school examination results', *Oxford Review of Education*, **19**(4) 425–33.

Gray, J. and Wilcox, B. (1995) *Good School, Bad School: Evaluating Performance and Encouraging Improvement*. Milton Keynes: Open University Press.

Greenwood, M. and Gaunt, H. (1994) *Total Quality Management for Schools*. London: Cassell.

Hargreaves, D. (Committee Chairman) (1984) *Improving Secondary Schools*. London: ILEA.

Hargreaves, D. (1995a) 'Inspection and school improvement', *Cambridge Journal of Education*, **25**(1), 117–25.

Hargreaves, D. (1995b) 'School culture, school effectiveness and school improvement', *School Effectiveness and School Improvement*, **6**(1), 23–46.

Hargreaves, D. and Hopkins, D. (1990) *Planning for School Development*. London: DfE.

Hargreaves, D. and Hopkins, D. (1991) *The Empowered School: The Management and Practice of Development Planning*. London: Cassell.

Hargreaves, D. and Hopkins, D. (eds) (1994) *Development Planning for School Improvement*. London: Cassell.

Heckscher, C. (1995) 'Defining the post-bureaucratic type', in Heckscher, C. and Donnellon, A. (eds) *The Post-Bureaucratic Organisation: New Perspectives on Organisational Change*. Thousand Oaks, Calif.: Sage.

Higher Education Quality Council (1994a) *Guidelines on Quality Assurance*. London: HEQC.

Higher Education Quality Council (1994b) *Learning from Audit*. London: HEQC.

Hofkins, D. (1995) 'Seven seek to make OFSTED accountable', *Times Educational Supplement*, 4 August.

Hopkins, D., Ainscow, M. and West, M. (1994) *School Improvement in an Era of Change*. London: Cassell.

Holly, P. and Southworth, G. (1988) *The Developing Schoool*. Lewes: Falmer Press.

Hutchinson, B. (1993) 'The effective reflective school: visions and pipedreams in development planning', *Educational Management and Administration*. **21**(1), 4–18.

Inner London Education Authority (ILEA) (1985) *Improving Primary Schools (The Thomas Report)*. London: ILEA.

Johnson, G. and Scholes, K. (1993) *Exploring Corporate Strategy* (Third Edition). Hemel Hempstead: Prentice Hall.

Joyce, B. (1991) 'The doors to school improvement', *Educational Leadership*, **48**(8), 59–62.

Keys, W. and Fernandes, C. (1990) *A Survey of School Governing Bodies*. Slough: NFER

Kohn, A. (1993) *Punished by Rewards*. New York: Houghton Mifflin.

Lewin, K. (1951) *Field Theory in Social Science*. New York: Harper & Row.

Louis, K. (1981) 'External agents and knowledge utilization: dimensions for analysis and action', in Lehming, R. and Kane, M. (eds) *Improving Schools: Using What We Know*. Beverly Hills, Calif.: Sage.

Matthews, P. and Smith, G. (1995) 'OFSTED: inspecting schools and improvement through inspection', *Cambridge Journal of Education*, **25**(1), 23–34.

Maychell, K. and Keys, W. (1993) *Under Inspection: LEA Evaluation and Monitoring*, Slough: NFER.

McGilchrist B, Mortimore, P., Savage, J and Beresford C. (1995) *Panning Matters: the Impact of Development Planning in Primary Schools*. London: Paul Chapman Publishing.

McHarg, D. (1995) MA assignment (quoted with permission). Institute of Education, University of London.

McLaughlin, M. (1990) 'The Rand Change Agent Study: macro perspectives and micro realities', *Educational Researcher*, **19**(9), 11–15.

McMahon, A., Bolam, R., Abbot, R. and Holly, P. (1984) *Guidelines for Review and Internal Development*. London: Longman.

McNiff, J. (1988) *Action Research: Principles and Practice*. Basingstoke: Macmillian.

Miles, M. and Ekholm, M. (1985a) 'What is school improvement?', in van Velzen, W., Miles, M., Ekholm, M., Hameyer, U. and Robin D. (eds) *Making School Improvement Work: A Conceptual Guide to Practice*, Leuven, Belgium: ACCO.

Morris, G. (1988) 'Applying business consultancy approaches to schools', in Gray H. (ed.) *Management Consultancy in Schools*, London: Cassell.

Mortimore, P. (1995) *Effective Schools: Current Impact and Future Potential*. London: Institute of Education.

Mortimore, P., McGilchrist, B., Savage, J. and Berisford, C. (1994) 'School development planning in primary schools: Does it make a difference?', Hargreaves, D. and Hopkins, D. (eds) *Development Planning for School Improvement*. London: Cassell.

Mortimore, P., Sammons, P., Stoll, L., Lewis, D. and Ecob, R. (1988) *School Matters: The Junior Years*. London: Paul Chapman Publishing.

Murgatroyd, S (1988) 'Consulting as counselling: the theory and practice of structural consulting', in Gray H. (ed.) *Management Consultancy in Schools*, London: Cassell.

Murgatroyd, S. and Morgan, C. (1993) *Total Quality Management and the School*, Buckingham: Open University Press.

Myers, K (Ed) (1995) *School Improvement in Practice: Schools Make A Difference*. London: Falmer Press.

NACETT (1995) *Review of the National Training Targets*. London: HMSO.

National Commission on Education (1993) *Learning to Succeed*. London: Heinemann.

Neave, H (1990) *The Deming Dimension*, Knoxville, Tennessee: SPC Press.

Newman, E and Pollard, A. (1994) 'Observing primary school change: through conflict to whole-school collaboration?', in Hargreaves, D. and Hopkins, D. (eds) *Development Planning for School Improvement*. London: Cassell.

OFSTED (1992; 1993; 1994) *The Handbook for the Inspection of Schools*, London: HMSO.

OFSTED (1994a) *A Focus on Quality*. London: OFSTED.

OFSTED (1994b) *Improving Schools*. London: HMSO.

OFSTED (1995) 'New framework for the inspection of schools' (Draft for consultation), OFSTED, February.

OFSTED (1995b) *Planning Improvement: A Report on Post-Inspection Action Plans*. London: HMSO.

OFSTED (1995c) *Inspection Quality 1994/1995*. London: OFSTED.

OFSTED (1995d) *Annual Report of Her Majesty's Chief Inspector of Schools*

Part 1: Standards and Quality in Education, 1993/94. London: HMSO.

OFSTED/Audit Commission (1995) *Lessons in teamwork: How school governing bodies can become more effective*. London: HMSO.

Ouston, J. (1993) 'Management competences, school effectiveness and education management', *Educational Management and Administration*, **21**(4), 212–21.

Ouston, J. (1995) 'Saving a baby from the bath water', *Management in Education*, **9**(2), 33–4.

Ouston, J., Fidler, B. and Earley, P. (eds) (1996a) *OFSTED Inspection: The Early Experience*. London: David Fulton Publishers.

Ouston, J., Fidler, B. and Earley, P. (1996b) 'Secondary schools' responses to OFSTED: improvement through inspection?', in Ouston, J., Fidler, B. and Earley, P. (eds) *OFSTED Inspection: The Early Experience*. London: David Fulton Publishers.

Parsons, C. (ed.) (1994) *Quality Improvement in Education: Case Studies in Schools, Colleges and Universities*. London: David Fulton Publishers.

Power, M. (1994) *The Audit Explosion*. London: Demos.

Preedy, M. (ed.) (1993) *Managing the Effective School*. London: Paul Chapman Publishing.

Pyke, N. (1995) 'Strugglers not sharing all top 52 successes', *Times Educational Supplement*, 10 February.

Reynolds, D. (1995) 'Some very peculiar practices', *Times Educational Supplement*, 16 June.

Reynolds, D., Jones, D. and St Leger, S. (1978) 'Schools do make a difference', *New Society*, 37, 321.

Riches, C. (1992) 'Inspecting the inspection of schools', *Management in Education*, **6**(2).

Riches, C. (1993) 'Building teams for change and stability', Unit 4 in Open University E326 Study Guide: *Managing Educational Change*. Milton Keynes: Open University.

Riches, C. and Morgan, C. (eds) (1989) *Human Resource Management in Education*. Milton Keynes: Open University Press.

Rosenholtz, S. (1989) *Teachers' Workplace: The Social Organization of Schools*. New York: Longman.

Russell, S. (1994) *Ready for Action: A Practical Guide to Post-OFSTED Action Planning*. Courseware Publications.

Rutter, M., Maughan, B., Mortimore, P. and Ouston, J. (1979, reprinted 1994) *Fifteen Thousand Hours: Secondary Schools and their Effects on Children*. London: Open Books. (Reprinted by Paul Chapman Publishing, 1994).

Sallis, E. (1991) 'Total Quality Management and Further Education'. Paper presented to BEMAS Conference, September.

Sallis, E. (1993) *Total Quality Management in Education*. London: Kogan Page.

Sammons, P., Hillman, J. and Mortimore, P. (1995) *Key Characteristics of Effective Schools*. London: OFSTED.

Sayer, J. (1993) *The Future Governance of Education*. London: Cassell.

Schein, E. (1988) *Process Consultation*, Volume 1 (Second Edition). New York: Addison-Wesley.

Schein, E. (1992) *Organizational Culture and Leadership* (Second Edition). San Francisco: Jossey-Bass.

Schmuck, R. and Runkel, P. (1985) *The Handbook of Organization Development in Schools* (Third Edition). Prospect Heights, Ill.: Waveland Press.

School Management Task Force (1990) *Developing School Management: The Way Forward.* London: HMSO.

Sengé, P. (1990) *The Fifth Discipline; The Art and Practice of the Learning Organisation,* London: Century Business.

Shaw, M. Brimblecombe, N and Ormston, M (1995) 'Teachers' perceptions of inspection: the potential for improvement in professional practice'. Paper presented to BERA conference, University of Bath, September.

Shearn, D. Broadbent, J. Laughlin, R and Willig-Atherton, H (1992) 'LMS and School Culture: the perceptions of Teachers, Heads and Chairs of Governors'. Sheffield University Management School Discussion Paper No. 92.40

Silver, H. (1994) *Good Schools, Effective Schools: Judgements and their Histories.* London: Cassell.

Steiner, G. (1979) *Strategic Planning: What Every Manager Must Know.* New York: The Free Press.

Stoll, L. (1992) *Making Schools Matter: Linking Schol Effectiveness and School Improvement in a Canadian School District.* Unpublished doctoral dissertation.

Stoll, L. and Fink, D. (1994) 'School effectiveness and school 'improvement: voices from the field', *School Effectiveness and School Improvement,* **5**(2), 149–177.

Stoll, L. and Mortimore, P. (1995) 'School effectiveness and school improvement *Viewpoint* 2, London: Institute of Education.

Swieringa, J. and Wierdsma, A. (1992) *Becoming a Learning Organization: Beyond the Learning Curve.* Wokingham: Addison-Wesley.

Tomlinson, J. (1993) *The Control of Education.* London: Cassell.

Vaill, P. (1991) *Managing as a Performing Art: New Ideas for a World of Chaotic Change.* San Francisco: Jossey Bass.

Van Velzen, W., Miles, M., Ekholm, M., Hameyer, U. and Robin, D. (eds) *Making School Improvement Work: A Conceptual Guide to Practice.* Leuven, Belgium: ACCO.

Wallace, M. (1991a) 'Development plans: an LEA solution causing a primary school problem?', *Education 3–13,* **19**(2), 39–46.

Wallace, M. (1991b) Contradictory interests in policy implementation: the case of LEA development plans for schools', *Journal of Education Policy,* **6**(4), 385–399.

Wallace, M. (1994) 'Towards a contingency approach to development 'planning in schools' in Hargreaves, D. and Hopkins, D. (eds) *Development Planning for School Improvement.* London: Cassell.

Watson, N. and Fullan, M. (1992) 'Beyond school district–university partnerships', in Fullan, M. and Hargreaves, A. (eds) *Teacher Development and Educational Change.* Lewes: Falmer Press.

West-Burnham, J. (1991) 'Total Quality Management in Education', in Bennett, N., Crawford, M. and Riches, C. (eds) (1992) *Managing Change in Education.* London: Paul Chapman Publishing.

Whittington, R. (1993) *What is Strategy and Does it Matter?* London: Routledge.

Index